Three Months Under the Snow

GREAT CHRISTIAN BOOKS
LINDENHURST, NEW YORK

Three Months under the Snow

The Journal of a Boy of Jura

Jean Jacques Porchat

Great Christian Books
is an imprint of Rotolo Media
160 37th Street Lindenhurst, New York 11757
(631) 956-0998

©2016 Rotolo Media / Great Christian Books

All rights reserved under International and Pan-American Copyright Conventions. No part of this book maybe reproduced in any form, or by any means, electronic or mechanical, including photocopying, and informational storage and retrieval systems without the expressed written permission from the publisher, except in the case of brief quotations embodied in articles or reviews or promotional/advertising/catalog materials. For additional information or permissions, address all inquiries to the publisher.

> Porchat, Jean Jacques, 1800—1884
> Three Months Under The Snow / by Jean Jacques Porchat
> p. cm.
> A "A Great Christian Book" book
> GREAT CHRISTIAN BOOKS an imprint of Rotolo Media
> ISBN 978-1-61010-039-7
> Recommended Dewey Decimal Classifications: 200, 240
> Suggested Subject Headings:
> 1. Religion—Christianity literature—Biographical
> 2. Christianity—Theology—Salvation
> I. Title

Book and cover design are by Michael Rotolo, www. michaelrotolo.com. This book is typeset in the Minion typeface by Adobe Inc. and is quality-manufactured on acid-free paper stock. To discuss the publication of your Christian manuscript or out-of-print book, please contact us.

Manufactured in the United States of America

JOURNAL ENTRIES

November 22nd,	11
November 23rd	18
November 24th	22
November 25th	24
November 26th	27
November 27th	29
November 28th	31
November 29th	32
November 30th	33
December 1st	34
December 2nd	36
December 3rd	36
December 4th	37
December 5th	37
December 6th	38
December 7th	38
December 8th	38
December 9th	39
December 10th	42
December 11th	42
December 13th	42
December 14th	44
December 15th	45
December 16th	46
December 17th	47
December 18th	49
December 19th	49
December 20th	52
December 21st	53
December 22nd	54
December 23rd	56
December 24th	57
December 25th, Christmas Day	57
December 26th	59
December 27th	60
December 28th	60

December 29th	61
December 30th	62
December 31st	64
January 1st, New Year's Day	65
January 2nd	67
January 4th	68
January 5th	70
January 6th	72
January 7th	72
January 10th	73
January 12th	74
January 13th and 14th	74
January 15th	85
January 16th	85
January 17th	86
January 18th	86
January 19th	86
January 20th	87
January 21st	87
January 22nd	87
January 23rd	87
January 24th	88
January 25th	89
January 26th	89
January 27th	89
January 30th	89
February 1st	90
February 2nd	90
February 3rd	90
February 4th	90
February 7th	91
February 8th	91
February 12th	92
February 13th	92
February 17th	92
February 18th	93
February 20th	93
March 2nd	95

INTRODUCTION

Young Friends,

The history which we present to you, under a title that may surprise you, is nevertheless founded upon truth. It would not surprise anyone who is acquainted with these mountainous countries, and the accidents to which their inhabitants are exposed.

Since this history has been put together not merely to amuse, but also to instruct you, we will describe in a few words the places where the circumstances happened, as well as the hard and laborious life of the inhabitants of the Jura. This will render the recital both more clear and more interesting to you.

The Jura is a chain of mountains formed of several parallel chains, running from Basle, in Switzerland, into France, and skirting the departments of the Doubs, the Jura, and the Ain, in a direction from N.N.E. to S.S.W. It is about 125 miles in length, and from 35 to 36 in breadth. The Jura contains a great number of valleys, and some of its peaks are of great height. Among these are distinguished *Le Reculet*, which is nearly 7000 feet above the level of the sea; the *Dole*, and *Mont Tendre*, which are above 6500 feet.

It is important to understand these details, because it is in a great measure the difference in the height of the mountains which renders them more or less habitable, for the atmosphere becomes colder in proportion to their height, and vegetation more scarce in proportion to the shortness of the summer; the snow descends upon them at a very early season, and there are some mountains so high that the snow never entirely melts upon them. But all the mountains of the Jura divest themselves of the snow every year; some vegetation is to be seen even on the highest peaks; on many points they are covered with magnificent forests of beech, oak, and particularly pines, while other parts offer excellent pastures, where they feed the finest cattle, oxen, sheep, and goats. Nevertheless, these fine mountains are not habitable for more than five months in the year, namely, from May or June until the beginning of October.

As soon as the snows are melted and the peaks begin to look green, the villages, all built in the valleys or on the lower declivities, send forth their flocks to the mountains. The day of their departure is a holiday, although the poor shepherds are going to banish themselves far from their families, during the whole of the fine season, to lead a hard laborious life, deprived of every comfort. During that time their chief diet is milk; they have only water to drink, and pass their whole time in feeding their flocks and making those large fine firm cheeses which are called *fromages de Gruyère*.

These are made on the mountain. There every shepherd has a châlet, a miserable house, most commonly built of stone. It is covered with strips of fir, called *bardeaux* or *tavillons* (shingles); large stones placed at intervals press them down with their weight, and prevent them from being carried away by the storms. The interior of the châlet is divided into three compartments: a well-closed stable to lodge the cattle at night; a narrow and cool dairy, where the milk is deposited in tubs of white wood; and a kitchen, serving at the same time for a bedchamber, where the poor herdsman has often nothing but straw for his bed. This kitchen has a vast chimney, under which there hangs an immense caldron, to heat the milk and convert it into cheese.

During the whole time of their remaining in the mountains, the herdsmen seldom see any person except a few strangers who are visiting the country. They willingly give them their cream, and receive in return a little new bread, a very rare delicacy in these châlets. However, these herdsmen never complain of their lot; they never wish to change their condition; they love their rude solitudes, and remain faithful to the customs, the labors, and the hearths of their fathers.

Their summer campaign does not end before the feast of St. Denis, the 9th of October. When they leave the mountain it is a holiday, like that of their departure from home, but much happier, because they are now going to revisit their families. Other labors of a different nature now begin at the village. These highlanders, whose only resource is in themselves, are very skillful; they make household utensils, tools, furniture; and cut and carve a number of articles from wood, which, being sold in the neighborhood, are carried to every part of Europe.

During their long winter days, the children study under the paternal roof, the way to the school not being always open and practicable. Gathered round their parents, many children acquire a taste for study, read together some interesting book, and thus instruct themselves while they amuse their family.

One young villager there is, not of an uncultivated mind, and we have therefore preferred letting him speak for himself. He will inform us how he was induced to draw up this journal, and how he found the means of doing it, when, by a train of circumstances with which he will acquaint us presently, he found himself with his grandfather imprisoned in a châlet.

We hope, young friends, that you may never be exposed to such severe sufferings; but in the course of your life you will often require patience and courage. The example of Louis Lopraz will convince you that even a child, who, by the grace of the Holy Spirit, puts his trust in God through Jesus Christ, is capable of exertions hardly to be expected at his age. You will learn that the school of affliction is often the most useful to a man, and that the Divine goodness shows itself as clearly to wards us in adversity as in prosperity.

"The boy is right," said my grandfather; "the snow is already so deep, and the wind so violent, that I foresee more danger in his going with you than in his remaining with me.

in return a little new bread, a very rare delicacy in these châlets. However, these herdsmen never complain of their lot; they never wish to change their condition; they love their rude solitudes, and remain faithful to the customs, the labors, and the hearths of their fathers.

Their summer campaign does not end before the feast of St. Denis, the 9th of October. When they leave the mountain it is a holiday, like that of their departure from home, but much happier, because they are now going to revisit their families. Other labors of a different nature now begin at the village. These highlanders, whose only resource is in themselves, are very skillful; they make household utensils, tools, furniture; and cut and carve a number of articles from wood, which, being sold in the neighborhood, are carried to every part of Europe.

During their long winter days, the children study under the paternal roof, the way to the school not being always open and practicable. Gathered round their parents, many children acquire a taste for study, read together some interesting book, and thus instruct themselves while they amuse their family.

One young villager there is, not of an uncultivated mind, and we have therefore preferred letting him speak for himself. He will inform us how he was induced to draw up this journal, and how he found the means of doing it, when, by a train of circumstances with which he will acquaint us presently, he found himself with his grandfather imprisoned in a châlet.

We hope, young friends, that you may never be exposed to such severe sufferings; but in the course of your life you will often require patience and courage. The example of Louis Lopraz will convince you that even a child, who, by the grace of the Holy Spirit, puts his trust in God through Jesus Christ, is capable of exertions hardly to be expected at his age. You will learn that the school of affliction is often the most useful to a man, and that the Divine goodness shows itself as clearly to wards us in adversity as in prosperity.

"The boy is right," said my grandfather; "the snow is already so deep, and the wind so violent, that I foresee more danger in his going with you than in his remaining with me."

THREE MONTHS UNDER THE SNOW

The journal of a young man of Jura

November 22nd, 1825

Since it is the will of God that I should be shut up in this châlet with my grandfather, I am about to write down daily whatever may happen to us in this prison; so that if we should perish in it, our relations and friends may know how we passed the latter days of our life; and that, if we are delivered by God's mercy, this journal may preserve the remembrance of our dangers and sufferings. It is my grandfather's wish that I should undertake this work, in order to shorten a little those hours which would otherwise seem tedious, and for which it would be difficult to find employment. I shall begin by relating what happened to us yesterday.

We had expected my father at the village for several weeks. St. Denis was passed, and all the flocks had descended from the mountain with their shepherds. My father alone did not return, and we all asked our selves what could have detained him. My uncles and my aunts assured us that we need not be uneasy; that perhaps there still remained some grass to be eaten, which was probably the reason why my father kept the herds some time longer upon the mountain.

My grandfather at length became alarmed at the delay; he said, "I will go myself and see what detains François; I shall not be sorry to pay another visit to the châlet. Who knows if I shall be permitted to do so next year? Will you come with me?" added he, looking at me.

I was just going to ask his leave to accompany him, for we were seldom apart from one another.

We were soon ready to start. We ascended slowly, sometimes threading the narrow passes, at others going along the side of deep precipices. At about a quarter of a league from the châlet, I had the curiosity to approach a steep declivity, and my grandfather, who had already told me that this made him uneasy, approached rapidly to take me by the hand; a stone which slipped under his foot caused a sprain, which gave him acute pain; but after some minutes he was able to walk, and we hoped that it would go off. By the help of his holly staff, and leaning upon my shoulder, he dragged himself hither.

My father was much surprised to see us. He was busy preparing for his departure; so that if we he had remained quiet at the village for one day longer, he would have arrived himself to put an end to our trouble.

"You, father!" he said, advancing to support him; "did you think that we had met with an accident?"

"Yes; we came to see what had detained you, when all our neighbors were returned."

"Some of our cows were ill; but they are now recovered. I shall send Pierre this evening with the remainder of the cheeses, and I intend to go down tomorrow with the herds."

"Are you very tired, Louis?" said my grandfather to me.

The tone in which he put this question showed me that he had some secret design, and I answered not very clearly.

"I was thinking," added my grandfather, "that it would be most prudent to send the boy with Pierre; the wind has changed within this half hour, and we shall, perhaps, have bad weather tonight."

My father expressed the same fear, and recommended me to follow this advice.

"If you wish it," said my grandfather, "I will go down with you; a short rest is all I require."

"I had rather wait for you," I said to my father, embracing him. "A whole night's rest is needful for Grandpapa, who has hurt his foot through my disobedience." I then related what had happened a short distance from the châlet; and it was agreed that we should all go down the next day, which was yesterday.

There was a pot upon the fire, which my father observed that I regarded with some degree of impatience. He served us from it with a soup made of the flour of maize cooked with milk, in a tureen, which we all ate, like soldiers, out of the same bowl; after which I went to bed. I fell asleep without paying much attention to the conversation of my grandfather and my father, who talked in a low voice for a long time after supper.

The next day, I was much surprised to perceive that the mountain was quite white. The snow was still falling in great abundance, and driven by a strong wind. This would rather have amused me if I had not observed the uneasiness which it caused my relations. I began to be uneasy myself when I saw my grandfather attempt to walk a few steps, and drag himself along with great difficulty, by leaning on the furniture and against the walls. The accident of the preceding day had caused his foot to swell, and he was in great pain.

"Go, go," he said; "take away this child before the snow gets deeper. You see that it is impossible for me to follow you."

"And do you suppose, father, that I can leave you here?"

"Place your son and the herds in safety first, and then you may think about me. You can return with a litter to take me away."

"Let me carry you on my shoulders, father, and let us set out without delay, I beg of you."

"My son, how are you to guide the flock and take care of this boy when so heavily laden?"

We thus passed a great part of the day without deciding upon anything. We were in hopes that someone would come from home to assist us. I said at length that I was big enough to do without a guide, and to help my father drive the herds. These representations were useless; my grandfather persisted in his resolution. He would not expose us to danger by encumbering us with his person.

My father pressed him eagerly and almost angrily. I wept. At length the dispute ceased, and I may say that it was chiefly by my interposition.

I said to my father, "Leave me also in the châlet. You will arrive the sooner at home, and you will return with assistance to take us away; grandfather will require someone to wait upon him and keep him company; and it will be an opportunity for me to testify my gratitude for all his kindness. We will take care of one another, and God will take care of us both."

"The boy is right," said my grandfather; "the snow is already so deep, and the wind so violent, that I foresee more danger in his going with you than in his remaining with me. Here, François, take this staff; it is very strong and armed with an iron point; it will help you to descend, as it assisted me in coming up. Bring the cows out of the stable; leave us the goat, and the provisions which remain. I am more uneasy about you than ourselves."

For a moment my father hung his head: looking up suddenly he caught me in his arms, and I felt his tears upon my cheeks. "I will not reproach you, my dear Louis, but you see the consequences of your disobedience: promise me not to be guilty of the same again. God has ordained what we see; and I must confess that neither your grandfather nor I foresaw the great embarrassment in which we are placed. If we had supposed last night that our situation would have been so sad today, we would have profited by the assistance of Pierre to take away grandfather."

"When I saw my father ready to set out, I presented him with a pretty bottle covered with straw, in which there remained a small quantity of wine, with which I had provided myself the day before.

"Take this," I said to him, "you will want it more than we shall today. You know that my poor mother gave me this bottle the first time that I came to pay you a visit in the mountain; I am glad that it is of use at a time of so much importance both for you and for us."

"Marie!" cried my father with emotion, "she is at rest!"

And he pressed me again in his arms in memory of one who was no longer able to caress me.

We brought out the herds, which seemed much astonished at finding the earth covered with snow. Some of the cows got away, and ran round the châlet. At length they were set forward on the way; and in a few moments my father disappeared in the thick clouds of snow with the flock.

Though they were no longer visible, my grandfather seemed still to follow them with his eyes. He leaned upon the window with out speaking, but his lips seemed to move, his hands were clasped, and his eyes lifted up to heaven. His attitude recalled me to a sense of my duty; I joined in his sentiments, and recommended my father to God. We had remained some time in this manner, when the wind began to blow with greater violence; thick clouds enveloped us, and the night fell almost suddenly. However, our wooden clock had scarcely struck three—

"Great God have mercy on him!" said my grandfather; "but he must have passed the forest some time, and he is not exposed to this whirlwind. He will be sadly uneasy on our account."

Our minds had been so occupied all day, that we had never thought of taking any food, and I was very hungry. At this moment I called my grandfather's attention to the bleatings of the goat.

"Poor Blanchette!" he said; "her milk is troublesome, and she is calling us. Light the lamp, we will go and milk her, and then have our supper."

"And our breakfast, too, Grandpapa!"

This made him smile, and I could perceive, by the light of the lamp, that he became more tranquil, which gave me a little courage. However, the wind roared violently. It rushed among the shingles, which shook with its force, so that we had some fear that the roof of the châlet would have been carried away. I lifted up my head several times.

"Fear nothing!" said my grandfather; "this house has sustained many similar assaults. The shingles are loaded with large stones; and the roof being nearly flat gives very little hold to the wind."

He then made me a sign to go before him, and we entered the stable. When my goat saw us, she redoubled her bleatings. She seemed ready to break her halter by the efforts she made to get to us. How greedily she ate the handful of salt that I gave her. Her tongue licked my hand over and over again, that she might not lose a grain. She gave us a good pailful of milk. I was in great want of it. My grandfather said to me when we returned to the kitchen, "We must be very careful not to forget Blanchette again; we must milk her punctually morning and evening; our life depends on hers."

"Do you think, then," I replied, "that we shall remain here a long time?"

"Perhaps so; but there is no knowing. We must always hope the best, and take precautions as if the worst were sure to happen."

After supper, I went and filled our nurse's crib, and gave her fresh litter. I caressed her, I must confess, more lovingly than usual; she seemed also more glad to see me. Goats are always fond of company, and she is now, poor thing, alone in the stable. When she saw me return to the kitchen, she began to bleat in the most plaintive manner.

We remained some minutes longer by the fireside; but we were far from being as well off here as in our house on the plain. The fireplace is as large as an ordinary room; it goes narrowing upwards, but the opening on the roof is so wide that the snow which entered it, driven by the wind, was very troublesome to us. It made a disagreeable noise, as it melted in the fire, and we were continually obliged to shake off the flakes with which our clothes were covered.

"You see, my boy," said my grandfather, "we shall get no warmth this evening, except in our bed. Let us go and take refuge there; the snow will not reach us in that shelter; tomorrow we will try and secure ourselves from it in the chimney corner. Let us pray to God, and seek his protection through our Lord and Savior; he is present everywhere, on the mountain as well as in the plain. Were the snow which covers us a hundred times deeper than it is, we should not be concealed from his sight; he sees our lifted hands, he hears our feeble sighs. Yea, Lord, thou art with us; we will rest without fear under the shadow of thy wings."

I was much affected, and never prayed with greater confidence than I did last night.

This morning, when I awoke, I found my self in complete darkness, and at first sup posed that my sleep had quitted me at an earlier hour than usual. However, I heard my grandfather feeling his way about, and I rubbed my eyes, but did not see a bit better.

"Grandfather," I said, "you are up before daylight."

"My dear boy," he answered, "if we were to wait for the light of day, we should remain long enough in bed. I fear the snow is above the window."

At this I uttered a cry of horror, and leaped out of bed. I soon lighted our lamp, and we were then able to perceive that my grandfather's conjecture was well founded.

"But the window is low," he added; "besides, it may be that the snow has been heaped up in this part; perhaps we should not see it above two feet deep at some paces from the wall."

"Then they will come to rescue us."

"I hope so; however, next to God, let us depend in the first place on ourselves. Sup pose it were his will to keep us shut up here for some time, let us see what resources we have; and when we have ascertained them, we will regulate the use we should make of them."

"There is no doubt that the day is come; the cuckoo clock* points to seven; it is fortunate that I did not forget to wind it up last night; this is a precaution we should be careful to observe. It is always pleasant to know how the time goes; and we must always be punctual with Blanchette."

Thus we began the day, which seemed sad and wearisome. I can no longer hold my pen; grandfather thinks I had better put off the remainder of my journal till tomorrow.

November 23rd —

If this continues I shall scarcely be able to write each evening the history of the day. When I was at school, I was often praised for the facility with which I executed the little compositions given as exercises to the higher classes; but I am far from being able to express, especially in writing, all I think and feel. I will, however, do my best. If these pages should ever be read by strangers, they must not forget that they were found in a châlet, and that they are the work of a schoolboy.

---

* The wooden clocks imported into this country are fabricated chiefly in the mountains of Switzerland, and keep very regular time.

Yesterday morning, when we discovered that we were closer prisoners than on the former day, we were very sad; however we did not forget our breakfast or Blanchette.

While my grandfather was milking her, I watched him closely and with great attention.

"You do well," he said, "you must learn to supply my place. You can see that I have some difficulty in stooping to this work. Come and try if you can milk her yourself."

After a short trial I succeeded in squeezing out a few drops of milk, but I believe I hurt our good nurse, for she started back and nearly overturned the milk-pail; I have, since that, both yesterday evening and this morning made two other trials, and have succeeded better.

After breakfast we examined what the châlet contained that might be useful to us. I will give an account of it another day, for fear I should be obliged to stop as I did yesterday.

When we had ascertained what we possessed in goods and utensils we were anxious to know the state of the weather. I placed myself under the chimney, and looked through the only aperture which remained free in the châlet. After some moments the sun shone out suddenly upon the snow, which now rose to a considerable height above the opening. I remarked this circumstance to my grandfather. We could easily distinguish the thickness of the layer of snow, because the opening has no chimney-pot above the roof. It is a mere hole like that of a hay loft.

"If we had a ladder," said my grandfather, "you could get up and unfasten a trap that your father has lately placed there, as he told me, to defend himself from the cold and rain till the chimney is repaired, which was in a bad condition when it was blown down.

"If the chimney were narrower" I replied, "I should not need a ladder, I could climb up like a chimney-sweeper."

We remained some moments in thought; suddenly my grandfather recollected that he had seen in the cow-house a long pole of fir, and reminded me of it. I clapped my hands with joy.

"That is all we want," I cried; "I have climbed many trees whose stem was no bigger. The pole has the bark on it still, which will make it the easier."

But we had to introduce it into the flue, and that occasioned some difficulty. Fortunately, however, the entrance to it was wide and very high, and we succeeded in our undertaking, being assisted by the flexibility of the wood.

I then set to work, having tied a string round my waist so as to hoist up a shovel when I was mounted. I succeeded by using my feet and hands, and leaning against the wall in getting upon the roof. I began by making room for myself by shoveling away the snow, and I then found it to be about three feet deep; round the châlet it seemed to me to be much more. The wind, indeed, had heaped it up, as they earth up vegetables to nourish them and prevent them from getting dry; but nevertheless an enormous quantity of snow had fallen in a very short time.

All the space that can be seen round the châlet is nothing but a white carpet; the forest of pines which surrounds it towards the valley, and which bounds the prospect, is white like the rest, except the trunks of the trees which seem quite black. Several of these trees have been broken by the weight of the snow; I saw large branches and even stems broken into splinters.

At this moment a cold icy wind blew from the north, the dark clouds which it drove before it opened at intervals and let the sunshine pass through them, and this dazzling light flitted over the snow with the swiftness of an arrow.

I was quite benumbed with the cold when I wished to explain to grandfather what I saw. He perceived that my teeth chattered; he told me then to make haste and to clear the trap by shoveling away as much snow as I could round the chimney. This labor took up much time, and gave me a great deal of trouble, but at the same time it warmed me. After having followed according to my grandfather's directions in everything, I replaced the cord in a pulley, so that the trap might be opened by pulling it down, and shut again by its own weight when the cord was loosened; this cord passed out of the flue and through the floor by means of holes made on purpose. After making two or three trials to assure ourselves of the complete success of the experiment, I descended much more easily than I had climbed up.

My clothes were quite wet, and I had no others. We lighted a bright fire with branches and cones of fir; then lowering the trap, and leaving only space enough for the smoke to escape, we passed a great part of the day in the chimney corner without any other light than the fire, for our provision of oil was very small, and it seems that we shall not very soon leave our prison. We only lighted the lamp when it was time to milk my goat.

It was a new and sad affair to linger out the day in this manner. I believe, however, that the hours would not have seemed so long had it not been for our prolonged hope of deliverance. I was always thinking that someone would come to our aid; I got up again upon the roof to see if there was any body coming, and never ceased questioning grandfather. He said that he hoped my father had got home in safety, but that perhaps the roads were rendered impassable, or the passes stopped up by the snow.

At length, after having quite closed the opening of the chimney, we went to bed yesterday, in the hope that someone would come to our aid today. Alas! we found out this morning that for the present the thing is almost impossible. It seems that it never ceased snowing all night. We had great difficulty in opening the trap; I succeeded at last, and we were able to light the fire. I discovered that the snow was two feet deeper than before. Grandpapa wishes me not to entertain any hopes of leaving this tomb before the spring. My own captivity is not that which saddens me the most; the dangers that my father has en countered, and, if he has escaped, his alarm on our account, trouble me much more.

Last spring I came here to pass some days with him, and I had brought, pens, ink, and paper with me, because he does not wish me to be quite idle when I cannot go to school. When I left him I wished to take away all that remained of these articles; but he said, "Leave all that in this cupboard, you will find it next year in good condition." This is the paper and pens which I am now using, very differently from what I expected.

November 24th —

I still tremble with horror when I think of the misfortune that nearly happened to us. Can it be believed that, buried as we are under the snow, we have narrowly escaped being consumed by fire? This is another danger which we have to guard against. We were sitting before the fire, and in order to pass away the time my grandfather was making me work some sums. I had spread the ashes on the hearth, as they do with sand in some schools, to trace the figures upon. While I was finishing my little sum we felt an unusual degree of heat behind us, it proceeded from a truss of straw which we were making use of for plaiting various articles, and which I had placed too near the fireplace. It was already on fire at one end. I wished to throw myself upon it to extinguish the fire, but I only burned my hands. Grandpapa, though he never can rise from his seat without pain, rushed to the truss and carried it off without a moment's delay, all flaming as it was, to the chimney.

"Remove," he said, "everything that can take fire."

I removed all the seats, the provision of wood, and everything that was near the fire place. We stood then for a moment aghast.

The flames continued to increase; we held the truss close against the wall of the chimney with the aid of a fork and a fire-shovel. We had not a drop of water to spare. The châlet was lighted up with the red glare; the smoke could not escape, and nearly suffocated us. Still, if we did not hold on, the truss would have fallen out and we should have been lost. Bits of lighted straw flew about on all sides; they might have fallen upon the bed in the corner of the room, or have set on fire the rafters over our heads, or else the partition which separated us from the cow house. A truss of straw ought not to take long in burning out, and yet I thought I should never see the end of it. At length, however, the flames subsided.

"Tread quickly," said my grandfather, "on what is still burning, and extinguish the least spark." He even set me the example himself. In a short time we were again plunged in total darkness, but we still continued in some degree of alarm till we had ascertained that the fire had not caught any part around us. The smoke, in its turn, gradually dispersed, we lighted the lamp and found ourselves as black as two coal heavers; but, thanks be to God, we were safe, both ourselves and our châlet having sustained no injury beyond the having slightly burned our hands and feet.

We shook off the ashes and dust with which we were covered, and my grandfather attributing the accident to his own negligence, said to me, "We can never be too quick in repairing our faults. If we had only a tub of water at hand we should have escaped this danger. We have a large empty cask in the dairy, we must take out one end of it and place it on the other near the fireplace. We will fill it with snow which will soon melt, and we shall have a provision of water in case of accident. Let us, in particular, be more careful and attentive. I need not tell you that the burning of the châlet would be our death; we have no means of escape; such an accident is as terrible for us as it would be for sailors on the wide ocean."

We set to work immediately. We opened the door of the châlet and filled the cask, after having placed it in a convenient situation. We shall be in no want of snow! I felt my heart sink within me, when I be held, on opening the door, that white wall which separates us from the whole world.

November 25th —

It is God's will that we should put our whole trust in him. The snow continues to fall abundantly. I have again had much trouble in clearing the trap which was load ed with it. We thought it prudent to clear the roof also from a part of the weight which was pressing upon it. I was employed for a long time at this work today. I left under my feet a layer of snow sufficiently thick to protect us from the cold, and I threw down the rest.

It is some relief to me to be for a short time out of our dungeon, and yet all I see around me looks very melancholy. One can scarcely now distinguish the unevenness of the ground round the house; the cistern, which I could perceive plainly yesterday, has now entirely disappeared; nothing can be more dismal than the landscape, the earth is white, the sky is black. I have read, at school, the account of voyages to the frozen ocean and polar regions; it seems to me as if we had been transported there. And since the wretched travelers who have suffered so much from the cold, and have encountered such great dangers, have sometimes returned to their country, I trust that we may also be permitted to see my father and our village again.

We are not altogether unprovided with necessaries in our sequestered abode. We have found more hay and straw than will be required for Blanchette for a whole year. If she continues to give us milk, we have a most precious treasure in her. But an unlucky circumstance might deprive us of her, and we have been very fortunate in finding a small provision of potatoes in a corner of the cow-house, which we must husband. We have begun by covering them with straw to protect them from the frost. In the cow house also my father had secured his stock of wood; but there is hardly enough remaining to warm us during a long winter. It is fortunate then that we thought of closing the trap at those times when we have no very urgent want of a fire; when there is a fear of being without fuel, we require other means of keeping out the cold. Happily the snow, by which we are imprisoned, serves to shelter us at the same time. I am surprised how little we feel the cold, buried as we are. "It is thus," said my grandfather, "that the corn is preserved so well under the snow." We shall do the same; we shall keep ourselves concealed all the winter, and, in the spring, we shall put our heads out at window; but till then it will be very tedious work, and God grant that it may all end well!

To supply the deficiency of wood we have a heap of fir cones, of which I had collect ed a great part myself to bum at home. Happily they had not been carried down to the village. If the worst comes to the worst, we can but burn the racks and mangers that are in the cow-house. In a case of life and death we do not look very narrowly into these things, it is only acting like sailors in a storm who throw their merchandise into the sea.

The châlet had been in great part unfurnished. What we regret least is the large caldron for making the cheese. They have left us some of the most needful cooking utensils, and moreover an axe, but all notched, and a saw which will scarcely cut at all. We have, each of us, a pocket knife. Scanty as our furniture is, we shall get on nevertheless. We regret most our provisions, for what we have are very miserable. What a pity it is that we could not find more than three of those loaves that are kept a whole year in the mountain, and at length broken in pieces with an axe. They were in an old oak tool chest which my father brought up here some years ago, because it took up too much room in the house; we have also found some salt, a little ground coffee, and a small provision of hog's lard.

"This is good," I said, when I found this last.

"Very much so," said grandfather, "but we must not apply it to the uses of our kitchen, it will serve for the lamp if the oil should fail us, and we have but little of it. Should you not prefer a poorer diet so as to have light?"

"Certainly," I replied; "how could we endure without it such nights as these, which set in at day-break?"

We have but one bed, but we sleep comfortably in it, according to the practice of the mountains; it is large enough to contain five or six persons. It is placed in a corner of the only room in the house, which is at the same time the kitchen and the cheese manufactory. Only one blanket has been left us; if that is not sufficient we have hay and straw, no sheets, no mattress, only a coarse straw one. I wish we had a more comfortable one for dear grandfather; a good bed makes an old man forget many other privations. For myself who could sleep upon the bare ground, and have often passed the night in a hay-loft, I have nothing to regret on this account. "I only wish," I replied, "that I had the instinct of the mice, and could sleep till the return of the fine season."

My grandfather immediately pointed out to me the folly and ingratitude of which I was guilty in expressing such a wish. He said to me, "Let us leave the brutes to enjoy such long sleeps; we have a better part to play. True it is God's will that we should suffer, but he has condescended to make himself known to us. Here is a splendid recompense for all our afflictions; accept it, my son, with gratitude, and fulfill the duties which it imposes on you. "Watch," he has said: "*for ye know not what hour your Lord doth come.*"

November 26th —

I could add to our inventory many articles which may be useful to us, but I shall not stop to enumerate them, for I hasten to relate a discovery which I have made, and which has occasioned to the two poor captives the greatest joy.

In examining into the state of our movables and provisions, I searched even the smallest nooks in the hope of finding some books. I knew that my father never went up the mountain without taking with him several religious works, in order to supply to the servants the place of Divine worship, which they were prevented from attending by the distance, by reading to them. But it seems that he had sent his little library back to the village.

We regretted much that in our solitary confinement we were deprived of this means of supporting and consoling ourselves during the tedious hours. Today, perceiving at the back of our oak chest, a plank which had lodged there, I drew it out, thinking that it might be of some use, and at the same time there fell out a book covered with dust, which had doubtless been mislaid for several years. It was *The Imitation of Jesus Christ*.

In recognizing this work, my grandfather cried out, "Here is a friend indeed come to visit us in our solitude! My child, the *Imitation* is a book written expressly for the afflicted; or rather it is a book which proves to us, in the most touching manner, that there is but one evil in the world, which is to forget God; and but one good, which is to love him. You see, dear Louis, if we are thus separated from the world, we are not forsaken; we have already found the means of sustaining the life of the body, we now possess that which will nourish the soul; nothing now remains, but to know how to make a good use of it.

"But observe, my boy, by what a succession of events we are led, first to feel the urgent want of the Divine assistance, and then to discover this help which had become so needful to us. Your father overstayed his time some days; we were uneasy, and wished to learn the cause of his delay. Had we waited one day longer, he would have returned; but we set out. You re member the accident which happened to me in the way, and which made it impossible for me to return the next day.

The snow fell, and we are prisoners. This was the point to which the Lord designed to lead us, in order to draw us nearer to himself. After having vainly searched for that of which we stood in such great need, a religious work, you have lighted by chance upon that which we despaired of finding. This is one example among a thousand of what are properly called, the ways of Providence. Indeed, it has so disposed all the affairs of this world, that one seems to spring out of another; that we are sometimes visited by joy, some times by grief, and always exercised by trial; for by these vicissitudes of life, in this succession of fortunate and unfortunate events, the character becomes formed: we are enabled to acquire those virtues which give dignity to the Christian; we approach gradually nearer to our model; we imitate Jesus Christ."

I answered, "I need not tell you how deeply I am touched by these reflections; you can perceive it yourself. Since we have been here, all you have said to me on the subject of my duty to God, strikes me in a new light. Till now, I have prayed that I might be able to follow your advice, and I yielded to it for the sake of pleasing you. Now I experience a new feeling with in me; I love the Lord most truly; my heart, at the thought of God, becomes softened, as it does when I think of you or of my father. Only, since this is a feeling to which I am not yet accustomed, and doubt less also because the idea of God is grand and awful, my love for him is blended with a deep sense of fear, which, although it troubles me, I rejoice in feeling. It is to you, grandfather, that I owe these happy dispositions, and I dare no longer regret the accident which has detained me here."

After having discoursed some time longer in this manner, we embraced one another, and remained silent a long time. I had never felt before so sweet and lively a sense of joy. Thus God changed evil into good; we derive happiness from affliction, and the afflicted are comforted.

Lord! thou hast drawn me to thyself by suffering; let me never forget Thee, when the day of suffering is passed. As thou at this moment teachest me resignation, so inspire me then with gratitude!

November 27th —

Always snow! It is seldom that so large a quantity falls at this season, even upon the mountains. Notwithstanding this, I did not cease to wonder why my father did not come to our aid, and I continued to express my surprise. Hitherto my grandfather would not allow himself to let me perceive his uneasiness; our conversation today has in formed me that he is not less alarmed than myself.

"This snow," I said, "has not come upon us at once; I should have thought that they could have opened a road here, either the first, second, or even the third day."

"I am very sure," said my grandfather, "that François has done all he could for us; it may be that he has not been able to impress his fears upon our friends and neighbors, and he alone could not deliver us."

"Do you think then that, having the power to take us hence, they would leave us here, with the risk of finding us dead in the spring? Have our friends and neighbors less humanity than those people of whom we read sometimes in the newspapers, and who expose themselves to the greatest labor, and even risk their lives, to rescue unfortunate beings who are buried in a mine, or a well, or under the rubbish fallen in an excavation?"

"I agree with you, that we are in a sad plight, dear Louis; but yet they know that we have a shelter and some provisions."

"But they know also that these may fail; that you are old and infirm, and that I have not yet the strength of a man; they ought to have some compassion on us."

"Perhaps they have made some attempts, and found it too difficult to proceed."

"However, if they want to open the high road when it is blocked up with snow, and form in its whole length a way large enough for carriages, they contrive to manage it, and that happens almost every winter."

"But this is ordered by the government for the public service, and is only done at a great expense."

"What then? Will they not do that to save two unhappy beings who are in danger of their life, which they can do for the mere convenience of travelers? This seems very cruel."

"The government likely has no knowledge that we are here."

"My father would not have failed to make it known, and to summon everybody to our aid."

Having said this, and finding that my grandfather remained silent, I added, taking both his hands, "Hide nothing from me, I beg of you. Is it not true that you entertain the same apprehensions as myself? Speak freely to me. Since I now know how to resign myself to the will of God, I am not unworthy of your confidence; tell me your fears, and do not let me remain longer a prey to my own; I had rather see my misfortune clearly, and know what you really think upon the subject."

"Well, dear Louis, I must own to you that I fear some accident has happened to your father. I must tell it you; besides, you have divined my thoughts. I am still much embarrassed about it; for besides your father, there are others who ought to have thought of us."

At this I began to weep and sob. My grandfather left me some time to indulge my grief. We sat before the fire, which went out. We remained thus in darkness till it grew late; my grandfather held one of my hands in his, and pressed it from time to time. "I have told you my fears," he said at length; "will you not let me tell you my hopes? We cannot foresee every thing. God's power surpasses all understanding. Be not cast down, but preserve yourself for the sake of your father and grandfather."

November 28th —

We have made as exact a calculation as we could of how much oil or grease our lamp burns in a day; and we have found that if it remains burning for twelve hours a day, our provision will be exhausted in a month. We have resolved, therefore, to limit ourselves to three hours of lamp light. The firelight will supply its place some times; but we can only allow ourselves this indulgence with economy; and yet it is a pity, for the fir wood produces a brilliant light, the blaze and sparkling of which please me much. While the lamp is not burning we converse. My grandfather has always something interesting to say to me, and I shall leave this place, that is, if our captivity lasts much longer, much more learned than I was. He has been for several years unable to work, and has passed all that time in reading good books, which a rich neighbor has lent him; I am now profiting by what he has read. He also gives me some lessons.

One of these, which shortens the time most, is working arithmetic by the head. He proposes little questions, and we try who can answer them the soonest. "When either of us is ready to give the solution, he tells the other, and we make use of this as a check. In this way an hour or two passes quickly. There is also emulation mixed with it. At first my grandfather had the advantage of me; so much so that in order not to discourage me he let me believe that he was puzzling at the solution, when he had already managed it. After a few experiments my attention improved; but he assures me that this is nothing to what I may yet acquire.

November 29th —

My journal is dated on a day which I must ever remember; for on the 29th of November I lost my dear mother; this is now four years ago. Last year the day fell on a Sunday. As we came out of church, I went with my father to the cemetery, and we stopped some time before the spot where the remains of our best friend are deposited. The grass was not yet withered by the cold; a few daisies were even in bloom, as it hap pens sometimes. I think I see them now waving in the wind, as if they meant to salute and thank us for our visit. We remained some time without speaking, at least with our lips; but our hands which were joined pressed each other, and spoke more than words could have done.

I did not live long enough with my mother to be acquainted with all her virtues; but the remembrance of her is fixed in our family, and constantly teaches us the greatness of our loss. Since her death, I do not think that my father has ever passed a day with out speaking to me of her. Sometimes he looks at me and discovers her likeness in my features; or, if I speak to him, instead of answering me, he says, "It seems to me as if I heard her speaking again."

My grandfather, now that he beholds me separated from both of them, is kind enough to be constantly reminding me of them in our conversations. He relates to me all that occurred at home before I was born; and even since, before I was able to know either myself or my parents. Ah! when he is upon this subject I want no other amusement; we can then put out the lamp, and wait patiently for the time of going to bed. Every thing which he tells me, and of which, perhaps, he would never have thought but for our misfortune, is engraved for ever in my mind.

Thus, then, I was for a long time the joy of my parents, without knowing or thinking of it! I gave them caresses which I no longer remember; I spoke to them in childish words which caused them the liveliest pleasure, but of which I can recall neither the time nor the occasion. These were the reward of all their cares and watchings. Upon this subject, my grandfather said to me, "How wonderful are the wisdom and goodness of Providence! It renders a child engaging, before he knows how to love himself; so that others are constantly guarding against the dangers that may happen to a being that has no fear for itself, and inter est themselves the more about it because it is unable either to think or provide for itself."

When I endeavor to recall raj earliest recollections, I see my grandfather at the corner of the fire, my mother in the garden, and my father coming in at the door with a fag got on his shoulders. These images become gradually more numerous and distinct, and I cannot help comparing these early days of my life with the early dawn of day. At first, the larger objects are only distinguished; gradually, every thing becomes visible, every thing becomes distinct, and our sight takes in the smallest objects.

November 30th —

We have found out a way of making use of our hands during part of the day, without burning more oil than prudence allows. As we have abundance of straws we plait them, or, rather, I braid them into long bands, which may serve numberless purposes. I have seen my father surround our beds of peas with similar bands to support them; they might, perhaps, be put to the same use for the corn, more especially the rye, which is more liable to be blown down; at least, when we can get the wood to make some chairs, we can make the seats of plaited straw.

I sit near the fire, and place myself so as to be able to work by its light; my grandfather watches my operations, and hands me the straws as I want them. He takes particular care that it shall not cause us any further alarm, and keeps it at a proper distance from the fire.

This occupation amuses us; it seems as if, while working for the fine season, we were bringing it nearer to us. Besides, it does not interrupt our conversation; my grandfather makes me relate what happened while I was at school, where I unfortunately sometimes found the time rather long. I like particularly to recall the visits of that good and rich neighbor, who used to come from time to time and distribute books as prizes to us. He used also to give us verses to learn by heart; this made the time pass more rapidly, especially when he recited these little poems, and explained their meaning.

December 1st —

I shudder in writing this date. If only a part of November has seemed so long, what will be the whole of the month we have now begun? But still more, will it be the last of our captivity? I dare not any longer look forward to its termination. The snow has accumulated to such a degree that it seems as if a whole summer would scarcely be enough to melt it. It now rises to the roof, and if I did not go up everyday to clear the chimney we should soon be unable to open the trap and to light the fire.

It is melancholy to think that my grandfather cannot, even occasionally, get out of this tomb. I asked him this morning what thing he desired most, and he answered, "a ray of sunshine." "However," he added, "our lot is much less unfortunate than that of many prisoners of whom several have not deserved their confinement more than we have. We have fire, we have often light, we enjoy a degree of liberty in our prison, and we find in it some means of amusement, which the four walls of a dungeon never present; we are not troubled everyday with the visit of an ungodly jailer, who is either absolutely cruel, or at least indifferent to sufferings.

The evils we experience by the will of God are never so bitter as those which we conceive that we may attribute to the injustice of men; in short, we are not alone, my boy; and if I am grieved that you should be shut up in this châlet, I will not conceal from you that your presence here supports me and is necessary for me. It seems too that you are not displeased with your companion; even poor Blanchette seems to soothe us in our imprisonment, and I assure you that it is not only for her milk that I am attached to her."

These last words set me thinking, and I proposed to associate this poor beast more nearly with us. "She is very lonely," I said, "she is always bleating; this might injure her, and consequently ourselves. Why should we not give her a corner here? The place is large enough for us all; she will thank us for doing her so much honor, and perhaps she will be a better nurse." This proposal was well received, and I immediately set to work. I arranged, in an angle of the kitchen, where it appeared the least likely to incommode us, a little manger, which I fixed to the wall with some large nails; I strengthened it with two posts, and without waiting any longer I brought Blanchette in to us.

How grateful she seemed for this change! She is as happy as can be, and constantly thanking us. If that were to last, it would be rather annoying. But when she gets accustomed to her new situation she will be more quiet than before. She is even now, while I am committing these details to paper, lying on her fresh straw; she is chewing the cud tranquilly, and looks at me with such a contented air, that she seems to guess that I am writing her history. She wants nothing now, and there is at least one happy being in the châlet.

December 2nd —

We forgot every thing after supper, but laying plans for our escape; and it is now so late that I have no time to write my journal. It would be always well filled and interesting, if I could repeat all the things that my grandfather says to me; but he prefers that I should rather write the history of our proceedings, than give a particular account of our conversations.

December 3rd —

Today, I was drawn out upon the roof by the bright sunshine. Dry cold weather has succeeded to the long fall of snow. How this white carpet dazzled me, and how beautiful the forest appeared! I hardly dared to tell Grandpapa all the pleasure I felt. By thinking a great deal, I have hit upon a scheme which, at first, appeared to me the most simple in the world, and I reproach myself for not having thought of it sooner. It is only to shovel away the snow from be fore the door, and to make a path with a gentle ascent, by throwing it up on each side. I have already set my hand to this work; my grandfather will soon see what he wishes for most—a ray of sunshine! I have worked all day; there is more work to do than I expected; but I should have done more if I had been permitted. My clothes are drying before the fire, and I have wrapped myself up in the blanket, while I note down in my journal the fortunate under taking of today.

December 4th —

The work goes on; I have continued at it as long as my grandfather would let me. He had conceived the idea of this job before I had, and I have scolded him for keeping it from me. He was afraid that I should suffer from the cold and damp, and was unwilling to tax the strength of his grandson for his own benefit.

December 5th —

We are now able to go out of doors. The path is made, and well trodden down; I have had the pleasure to see my grandfather walk over it, supporting him myself on one side while he leaned on the other on a rail, which I had fixed at one end to the house, and at the other to a post sunk in the snow.

We remained some moments at the top of our avenue, which is not very long; but the day was gloomy, and we felt ourselves very sad at seeing that black forest, that cloudy sky, and that snow which environs us with the silence of death. One single living creature appeared in sight; it was a bird of prey, which passed by us, uttering a hoarse cry. He reached the valley, and flew in the direction of our village.

"Among the heathens," said my grandfather with a sorrowful smile, "they would have given a meaning to this bird, his flight, and his cry; superstitious men would have found a subject for fear or for hope in his appearance. Shall we soon follow the direction in which this bird has flown? God only knows; he is too good and too wise to make our fate known to us; or if it were his will to do so, he would not make use of a brute as his prophet. Come, dear Louis, let us await his pleasure. I thank you for the trouble you have taken for me; I will take more advantage of it another day."

We went in; and, contrary to my expectations, we were more serious than usual, in spite of all our efforts. Thus, the result does not always respond to our hopes. The gloomy weather is not sufficient to explain our sadness; I think it is caused by the very fact of having been able to go out, of having imagined ourselves at liberty, and yet feeling that we are as much prisoners as we were before.

December 6th —

One idea gives birth to another. This time it was my grandfather who spoke first; he knew that I should benefit as much as himself by the proposal. He has employed me to clear away the snow from before the window. It will require time, because there is a much more considerable quantity in this part; besides, to gain our end in obtaining light there must be a much greater slope on both sides. I have commenced operations without suffering my grandfather to have anything to do with them. He has not insisted upon it, knowing of how much value his health is to me. "I will not," he said, "expose you to the least embarrassment, to give myself a little amusement."

December 7th —

We are less forward than yesterday; the snow has begun again, and the wind is so cold, that I have not been allowed to work out of doors. I have today only cleared away the snow that had recently fallen be fore the door. I must retain what I. have done; everything requires to be kept up, and I will not fail for want of perseverance.

December 8th —

The weather was milder today, and I resumed our work; but an accident has happened to me, at which I only laughed at first, though the consequences might have been very serious. I had already cleared away a great deal of snow, and thought I was drawing near the end of my task, when a heap of snow which I had thrown up over my head rolled down upon me and completely buried me. My grandfather, who had just returned into the châlet, had no fears, because he had given me proper directions to guard me against this accident; I had neglected them, and did not call to him at first for fear of alarming him; I hoped to be able to extricate myself. I succeeded, in fact, in getting my head out, but it was all I could do without assistance. After having struggled a long time in vain, because the snow afforded me no safe and solid footing, I was forced to call to my grandfather to help me.

He came in the greatest alarm, and dragged himself with much difficulty to the place where I was almost buried alive. When by his aid one of my arms was free, I was soon set at liberty; but I shall hardly be allowed to continue this work, of which my own carelessness alone has prevented the complete success.

December 9th —

May the Lord have mercy upon us! We have just passed the most dreadful day of our captivity. I never knew before what a hurricane was upon the mountains. Even now I cannot tell what has happened out of doors. We first heard the most frightful rumblings; when we attempted to open the door, we beheld clouds of snow flying with such rapidity, and the wind rushed with such violence into the châlet, that we had the greatest difficulty to close it again so as to fasten the latch. We were obliged also to let down the trap; and then we could have no fire, because the smoke entirely filled the room.

We remained a long time in the dark after having milked Blanchette, and breakfasted on her milk without boiling it; only before putting out the lamp we read a few pages of the *Imitation*. Then my grandfather supported my courage by his serenity; his grave and pious words mingled in the darkness with the howlings of the storm. At the very moment when one might have thought that the curse of God was upon us, he spoke to me only of his mercy.

"That same power," he said, "which seems to us so terrible today, will soon appear to us full of gentleness and love; it seems now to threaten all nature with total destruction, and we might suppose that we were again to be involved in that chaos in which all matter existed before the Lord said, "Let there be light." How blind we are! These tempests only prepare the way for a new creation. You will again see the plains, my boy, in all their verdure, the harvest lands covered with gold; your eyes will wander again over flowering orchards, and look up to the expanse of heaven, all brilliant with light. Will this wonderful change cause you to acknowledge the omnipotence of God? Shall you learn to love him then even as you fear him now? After having seen with what terrible effects nature raises upon the mountains these heaps of fertilizing waters, which she sends afterwards in copious streams into the valleys; after having learned to understand the views of Providence in this respect, will you learn also to bring your weak intelligence into subjection to his infinite wisdom? Will you then understand that prudence as well as respect and meekness bid us rely upon that wisdom? If such should be the effect of our sufferings, the dreadful day we are now passing ought to be considered as the happiest of your life."

With such exhortations as these my grandfather engaged my attention, and supported my courage. We were seated on our bed, and had spread over us a truss of straw. My grandfather, perceiving that I was drowned in tears, passed one of his arms round my neck, and, joining his hands upon my breast, held me for some time in his embrace with out speaking. At length when he perceived that I had become calmer, and that I had not waited for the abatement of the storm to recover myself, he said:—

"Well, do you mean to let me have all the conversation to myself? Have you no answer to make? Have you not presence of mind enough to express your thoughts?"

"Do not think me so unreasonable," I replied. "My feelings and my tears do not come from a weak and cowardly heart, so unworthy of yours."

I had hardly uttered these words, when there came a gust of wind more violent than any which had preceded it, and we heard the door crack with such force as to make us both start; my grandfather, after having said a few words to encourage me, remained silent for a moment, and then said:—

"As we have no fire today, we may recompense ourselves by having the light burning a little longer than usual; besides, it might be as well to see what can have shaken the door, and if any accident has happened, to repair it immediately."

We were up directly, and after having lighted the lamp, we discovered, on half opening the door, that an immense mass of snow had fallen against it, so that we are now shut up as completely as before. This was a subject of great regret to me, but I had now learned to submit without murmuring to this new disappointment.

"Consider," said my grandfather, "that if the storm had surprised us before the châlet was buried in the snow, it would not perhaps have been able to stand against it. Let us receive with submissive resignation this order of things, to which we owe our escape today from very great danger."

The tempest continues while I am writing. We have contrived to boil our milk with some fir cones. This sort of fire produces very little smoke, and fills the châlet with an agreeable resinous odor. We have been able to warm ourselves a little; and having just read a few pages of our excellent counselor, we hope, by God's blessing, to obtain a little sleep upon our straw.

December 10th —

We have heard less wind today; but we know not the state of the weather; we think, however, that the snow still falls in great abundance; at least the trap is so loaded with it, that with all my efforts I cannot open it. We are reduced to the necessity of burning nothing but cones, for fear of being suffocated with the smoke. I have contrived however, in order to give us a little more light, to split some logs of fir into slight laths, which I light at one end; these burn of themselves for some moments: but how I regret my window! It is now hidden as completely as before. I must decidedly, when the weather will allow, make another attempt to give us a little light, and a little liberty.

December 11th —

The cold is much more severe. Although we are buried in the snow, which, perhaps, prevents our hearing the storm, we feel frozen to the very bones; so that, in order to avoid suffering in one way, we are obliged to submit to it in another by involving our selves in a cloud of smoke. Unfortunately Blanchette seems to bear this with less patience than ourselves; and yet we cannot think of removing her to the cow-house, where she would be cold and solitary.

My grandfather assures me that the cold must be very intense, in order to make itself felt to such a degree in a house so shut in as this is on all sides. He supposes that the wind has changed to the north.

December 12th —

We had a dreadful alarm yesterday; today even I can scarcely collect my thoughts enough to write down what has passed. Alas! we are not yet sure that we have escaped all danger.

I was busy milking my goat while my grandfather was lighting the fire. Suddenly, she pricked up her ears, as if she heard some extraordinary noise, and then began to tremble all over.

I observed this at once, addressing myself to her—

"What is the matter, poor Blanchette?"

I said, caressing her; but immediately we heard the most dreadful howlings, as it were over our heads.

"Wolves!" I exclaimed.

"Silence, my boy! caress Blanchette," said my grandfather; and he approached her himself, and gave her some salt. She continued to tremble, and the howlings continued also.

"Well, Louis," he said in a low voice, "what would have become of us, if you had opened a passage to the window? Who knows if even the chimney might not have afforded a passage to these ravenous beasts?"

"And do you think we are safe, even as we are?"

"I hope so; but speak low, and do not cease to caress Blanchette, her bleating might betray us."

One would have thought that she had the same fears, for she did not make the slightest noise. My grandfather came and sat down by me; I held my goat in my arms; he had his hand laid upon my shoulder, and I needed all the encouragement of his calm and serene countenance, to keep me from shrieking aloud with fright.

All that I had previously experienced in the châlet could not be compared to the agony of yesterday, throughout the whole day. We passed it by the side of Blanchette, and at several intervals we heard the howlings of the wolves; at one time it was so loud, that I thought my last hour was come.

"They're digging through the snow," I cried, clasping my grandfather in my arms; "they will surely get in and devour us."

"I would not deceive you, my boy; if our situation is painful, I do not think it is by any means dangerous. These wolves may be running over the mountain, because the surface of the snow is frozen hard; but they will not remain long upon the heights. At this season, they resort to the neighborhood of the plains and villages. Perhaps they have brought the carcass of some animal here, and make this outcry that we hear because they are quarreling while they devour it."

"Even if they should succeed in discovering that we are here, they could never penetrate through the roof and the ceiling; they would never guess the situation of the window, nor could they lift up the trap: the worst they can do is to annoy us with their cries. Let us here again, my child, ac knowledge the goodness of God. The storm which He ordained for us yesterday, has been our preservation: He has repaired, in the destruction of your labors, the mis chief that our imprudence had caused; He has shut out from us the light you wished us to enjoy, but it will be the saving of our lives. What a blessing it was that these wolves did not come upon us while you were working out of doors! We must be more on our guard in future."

"Then," I said sorrowfully, "our captivity will become more painful. The winter is only just beginning; the cold may become more severe; we shall never get out of this place."

Such was the conversation we held all day. Till night we heard these savage wolves. At length we went to bed; but I scarcely slept at all, though the howlings had entirely ceased.

Today I thought I heard them again; my grandfather assured me that I was deceived. It is certain that Blanchette trembles no more; she eats, chews the cud, and sleeps as usual, and we think that since she is quiet we may be the same.

December 14th —

Since this new danger has threatened us, of which I never thought before, I feel my self sad and cast down. It is not only the horrible idea of being torn in pieces by wolves which haunts me, it is the thought that I shall not be able as formerly to quit my prison for a few moments, and breathe the open air; and also the necessity of giving up all idea of clearing the door and window, which would have rendered our situation more endurable.

Before this new accident, I had drawn for myself almost a delightful picture for the future. I hoped to restore to my grandfather the sight of the sun; we were enjoying from the window a small degree of light; we were amused sometimes with external objects; it seemed as if I were waiting, without too much impatience, the thawing of the snow and the moment of following the streams into the plain.

Now what a difference! We no longer know what is passing outside of the châlet; it is become uncomfortable by the smoke; and the only way to free ourselves from this restraint is to risk our safety. God grant that this increasing anxiety and prolonged confinement may not make either of us ill!

My grandfather sees my depression, and blames me for it; he reminds me of the sentiments which I expressed some days ago; he finds me so different from what I was, that he scarcely recognizes me. I am much of his opinion I confess; and if I go to bed afflicted at my lot, I am still more dissatisfied with myself.

December 15th —

Today is Sunday. What are our friends and neighbors doing this evening which we are passing so sadly? Are they thinking of us? Yes, certainly, if my poor father is still among them; but if he has fallen, in endeavoring to release us perhaps, the others have already forgotten us: we are dead to all the world. They are enjoying in the village the repose of winter; they are consuming, gaily, the autumnal fruits; they are paying visits; they pass the evening round a bright fire or a warm stove. I have never felt till now how much other men are necessary to our happiness. They divide their labors, and they are less painful; they share their pleasures, and they double their value.

Oh! if God should be pleased to restore me one day to the society of my brothers, how I shall enjoy it! What a pleasure it will be to hear the sounds and see the bustle of the village! what happiness to feel that we are surrounded by neighbors who love and protect us! what delight in rendering to one another mutual offices of kindness! But our friends must know what we are suffering here; can they leave us willingly in this dreadful state of abandonment?

"Do not dwell, this evening at least," said my grandfather, "upon such a painful thought; it is a bad way of concluding the day that is consecrated to God. If men forget us, let us forgive them, in order to obtain pardon of Him whom we are too often forgetting. You regret the society of your companions; that of your heavenly Father ought to be sufficient to give you both joy and peace."

"You must assist me, my revered friend," I replied, "to recover those pious sentiments which animated me before I found myself exposed to so dreadful a death. Grant me, O God, the virtue of thy holy martyrs, who were able to bless thee in the face of the most horrible tortures! If I am to sacrifice my life to thee in this place, give me the courage to do it with firmness! Even children have been known to glorify thee in the midst of torments."

December 16th —

Our whole diet consists of goat's milk, pieces of dry hard bread, and boiled potatoes which we eat with a little salt. Still we are obliged to be very sparing of our potatoes, for our stock is small. Sometimes, for a change, we roast them in the ashes, which we like best.

Until now my grandfather has never been willing to touch our coffee; he has at length resolved to do so, in order to endeavor to regain his appetite. Our late alarms have affected his health. This little treat, in which he consented to indulge at my earnest request, has done him good. He wishes me to share it; but I have positively refused. It must be reserved for cases of absolute necessity, and I do not stand in any need of it whatever.

A milk diet ought certainly to be sufficient for a man's nourishment. The shepherds of the Alps live entirely upon it for a great part of the year; and people who eat bread and meat and drink wine are not always so strong and healthy; but in our villages they have a little more variety. Besides, it is more difficult for an old man to change his manner of living, and I am grieved to see my grandfather reduced to live upon Blanchette's milk.

For himself, he will not allow me to pity him; and when I was telling him this evening how much I suffered by his privations, which were originally caused by my disobedience, he interrupted me, and begged me never to touch upon that subject again.

December 17th —

"Time passes, and the winter is approaching," said my grandfather today.

"Approaching?" I cried; "is it not already come?"

"Not yet by the almanac. Winter only begins on the 21st of December; till then we are in the autumn."

"True; I remember that our school master thus explained the divisions of the year. Can it indeed be said that we are still in the season of fruit?"

"My child, even in the valley the harvest has been gathered in a long time, as you know; and on the mountains the winter begins sooner."

"And ends later," I replied, sadly.

"Yes; but it may become mild enough for us to be delivered before the return of spring. Only let a warm south wind blow for a few days, and all this snow will melt faster than it has fallen."

"What a slender thread our life hangs upon!"

"Does that surprise you? From the very moment of your birth you have been in the same dependent position. We live surrounded by danger, which we very often are unaware of; and that which the circumstances in which we are placed may add to it, is a mere trifle. Accustom yourself, my child, to this reflection, that at every moment of our lives an unforeseen accident, often the most trifling in appearance, may put an into them. Thus you will learn to be cautious when you think you are in the most perfect safety, and firm when surrounded by the greatest dangers."

To this exhortation of my grandfather I answered, as I often did, by opening the *Imitation of Jesus Christ*, in order to read to him a passage which bore relevance upon what he had been saying to me.

"When it is morning," so the book expresses itself, "reflect that you may never see the evening; and when it is evening, never rely upon the certainty of seeing the morning. Always, therefore, be ready, so that death may not take you unawares. Many people die by a sudden and unforeseen death; for 'the Son of man cometh at an hour when ye think not.' "

"I am pleased to observe," said my grandfather, "how this book becomes familiar to you. If you continue to study it, it will stand by you as a real friend; it will often respond to your thoughts; it will be your counselor in times of difficulty; it will con firm your own reflections by its respectable authority; and, as you will find it often agreeing with you, it will give you such confidence in your own strength as you may reasonably hope for."

"Such, my child, is the use which we ought to make of a good book. And I as sure you many people have well-furnished libraries, who know not how to derive any advantage from them; because in reading they only seek for amusement, instead of assistance in the daily conduct of their lives. They live to read, instead of reading to live. Try to avoid following their example."

December 18th —

My grandfather has eaten almost nothing all day; he has tried again the mixing of a little coffee with his milk, of which he swallowed a small quantity; he consented also, at my earnest entreaty, to dip a little bread in it; he has made efforts which he could not conceal from me, to appear as calm and serene as usual; I was much affected by it, and it did not lessen my anxiety. If he should fall ill, now that our situation becomes daily more difficult and distressing, O God, in what need shall we stand of thy help! I implore it with all my heart, but resign myself entirely to thy will.

December 19th —

Why should I complain of the difficulties which surround me, when each one serves as a spur to my mind, and stimulates my courage? The smoke has caused us so much suffering, that we long to open the trap, were it possible, by clearing away the snow which covers it; on the other hand, the fear of the wolves restrains us from it. Well! I have today thought of a plan to effect what we want; we can now make a fire, and have even done so, without being annoyed by the smoke, and without exposing ourselves to the attacks of our fearful enemies.

My grandfather complained of numbness, which I attributed to the want of a fire; for we could not rely upon what we obtained from the cones, when we were obliged to limit ourselves to the feeble supply of warmth we received from them. I had observed in a corner of the cow-house, where we keep our little stock of potatoes, a rusty tube of iron; I knew that it had belonged to a small stove with which the châlet had been warmed last year, but which has now been removed.

"Could we not," I asked, "fix this tube in the trap, by making a sufficient opening in it?"

"It is a good thought," replied my grandfather; "but there are are many difficulties in the way of executing your plan. How are we to make the opening? How can you fix yourself up there to work at it? It can not be done without danger, and I will not allow you to expose yourself to the risk of a serious accident, only to save me from a slight inconvenience."

I remained silent, but began to think. I knew that it would be useless for me to urge the matter, until I had hit upon some plan to assure my grandfather of my safety.

I saw at once that the hole might be made in the trap without difficulty. The plank is not very thick, and one of our knives has a very good small saw attached to it. Some days ago, I found a gimlet in the drawer of the table; very blunt indeed, but not so much so as to prevent its boring a hole in a deal plank. A hole once made with this, I could introduce and work the saw, and then remove a round piece of wood, of the size of the tube.

But how could I secure a firm footing while doing the work? I happened to have a strong new cord; this I tied firmly to the upper part of the pole, leaving, lower down, two looped ends, like stirrups, for my feet to rest in when I had climbed up. As a further assistance, I took another end of the rope to fix it to the ring of the trap and fasten it round my waist.

After having explained to my grandfather how I meant to set to work, I obtained his leave to begin; and I had laid my plans so well, that, at the first trial, the tube passed through the opening, when I fixed it with some nails driven through the edge, which I had previously pierced with holes at equal distances.

I came down quite happy. I removed from the fireplace the snow which the tube had cut through in its ascent, and I had the satisfaction of seeing the smoke of a sparkling fire, which I lighted, ascend with out difficulty.

This was a whole day's work; but allowance must be made for the indifference of the tools, the awkwardness of the situation, and, above all, the inexperience of the work man. I do not, however, deserve all that my grandfather would say to reward my labor. I am more than repaid by the pleasure of seeing him with his feet on the dogs, enjoying the brightness of the fire, and warming himself before he goes to bed.

After reading the foregoing details, my grandfather insists upon my writing down what he is going to dictate. The following are, therefore, his words:—

"I do not know what the future has in store for me; but I wish, if possible, to make known every one of the motives which I have to bless God for having placed me in this apparently so dismal prison. My grand son always speaks with becoming modesty of what he has done, and I shall be careful not to wound his humility by saying too much in his praise. 'The praise of men,' says the wise author whose lessons we study everyday with increasing pleasure, 'does not serve to make us more holy; we are but what we are; and all that men can say of us, can never make us greater in the sight of God.' But if the conduct of my grandson has filled my heart with joy, I may at least allow myself to testify it to him, especially if I refer to God the glory of all that I behold this child doing for the sake of his grandfather."

"Yes, my son; to God alone be the glory! You looked up to him, from the first, in the performance of your duties. Today, for example, all the time that you devoted yourself to this difficult task, which has been of such benefit to me, has, doubtless, been with you a time of prayer. While your hands were working with all their strength, your young heart was lifted up to God with all the ardor of your age; you prayed to him that success might crown your endeavors. Happy employment of life! Thus ought we always to work. Let us again quote the words of our wise friend.

"'Bodily occupations often draw the soul along with them, and prevent it from retiring within itself, and thinking enough upon God; but when we apply ourselves to bodily labor with the sole view, in performing them, of fulfilling the will of God, then the mind is not distracted by them; and by all our different employments, one single object is attained, which is to seek to please God.'

"Grant, O Lord, to the old man that wisdom which he is seeking to instill into this child! If thou art making use of me as an instrument to draw my grandson to thyself, continue, I beseech thee, to make him an instrument of salvation to me! Thus blessed be my trial, and blessed be the captivity to which thou hast condemned me together with him! I refuse nothing, O Lord, which thou seest good for me. I accept all these sufferings, if they can serve to bring us nearer to Thee."

December 20th —

"I do not wish," said my grandfather, "to alarm you unnecessarily; but I think we should do right to take some precautions against the wolves, in case, which is not very likely, they should return and find out our only window. This opening is not very securely closed; the framework is old and weak, it would not resist the attacks of the enemy, therefore let us try to fortify our citadel in this point."

The freestone in which the frame is set is sufficiently soft; we have wrought two holes above and two below, with the aid of a pointed iron which we use instead of a chisel; we have fixed in these holes two bars of oak, taken from the mangers where they were useless. For greater security we have placed outside against these bars some planks, fitted, as well as we could do them, into two grooves, open on each side. Now we have no more fear of an invasion by the window than by the door.

For the latter we keep it constantly latch ed and bolted. We only open it with great precaution, when we want to lay in a stock of snow; for we only use thawed snow for all our household purposes, and we have not yet observed that it is less wholesome than common water.

December 21st —

We are careful of our oil, and our economy in this respect has nearly occasioned the loss of a large jar in which we keep our water for drinking. But here again good has come out of evil as will be seen. The jar was placed in a corner; in searching for something in the dark, I knocked it over. Happily the floor of the châlet is nothing but beaten earth, so that the jar was not broken.

"We will prevent any future accident of the same kind," said grandfather. "Dig a small hole in this corner, where the jar, whose base is too small with respect to its height, can be set more safely."

I had lighted the lamp to do so, and had taken a pick-axe for the purpose; but just as I was about to strike the first blow,— "Stop!" said my grandfather eagerly, as if a sudden thought had come across him. Then he drew near and took the tool out of my hands, with which he began to pick the ground, but very lightly and carefully. I asked him what he was looking for; for I clearly perceived by his manner of working that he was more afraid of breaking something hidden in the ground, than desirous of finishing the work which he had at first employed me to do.

"Ah! I did not deceive myself, my dear boy," he said, showing me a dusty bottle. "At the very moment you lifted your arm I suddenly remembered that, years ago, I had deposited in this same spot four or five bottles of wine left over from that summer's provision. I had all but forgotten them. Put this one upon the table; we have only now to look for the others. There are only a few more, I am certain; but, my dear Louis, I look upon this as a most fortunate discovery.—Look, here are the second and the third."

Well, we found five in total, and I pressed Grandpapa to taste it immediately. What a pleasure it was for me to pour for him a glass of this old wine! The meager diet to which he has been reduced for the last month, renders this cordial absolutely necessary to him; but he would not take more, considering this beverage as a remedy that ought to be rationed. I was obstinate in refusing to take any of it, having no occasion for it on account of any malady whatever.

"At least moisten your lips in honor of the day," said my grandfather; "it is the last day of the vintage season, or, if you prefer it, the first of winter. The sun is about to return in its course and come nearer to us; the days will now grow longer, at first scarcely perceptibly, it is true; but it is like the return of hope, we should welcome it with joy."

I did as he desired me, and then put aside with great care this unexpected provision, which I hope will have a good effect upon the health of my aged parent.

This little incident restored our courage, and we chatted together a long time. My grandfather gave me a lesson in astronomy; and I think I now understand well how the earth moves round the sun, how the night and day are caused, the winter and summer, the spring and autumn.

December 22nd —

I have learned from geography that the inhabitants of the mountains have distinct manners and customs. "And we ought not to be surprised at it," said my grandfather, "when we observe how different their way of living is from that of other people. The mountaineers are confined for a great part of the year to their solitary huts; and when they leave them with their flocks, it is again for solitude. A shepherd of the Alps en joys less of the society of men in a year, than the inhabitants of our villages do in a month.

"This solitary life must necessarily produce a marked effect upon the character. A man is thrown more upon himself; he lives, as it were, upon his own reflections; he is accustomed to depend upon his own strength to contend with difficulties which present themselves in a state of uncultivated nature. This life of hardship tends to the formation of patience and religious feeling. It is almost the life of those hermits who are represented to us as passing their days in continued austerities and in silent contemplation."

These were my grandfather's words, which, as he spoke by the light of our fire, made him appear to me like one of those holy men who were the objects of public veneration in ages past. His beard began to cover the lower part of his face; he wears a cap trim med with grey fur, his brown coat is made of the coarsest cloth; his costume forms a singular contrast to his mild look and gentle smile. Sometimes I remain a long time looking at him; and when I think of all that he must suffer, whether on my account, or by the infirmity of age, my eyes are filled with tears.

But we are careful to divert each other from our sorrowful reflections. My grandfather is always anxious to converse, and I endeavor to make it agreeable to him by my docile attention, being unable to repay in kind the instructions of my venerable parent. Today he entertained me with an account of the works to which the mountaineers of the Alps and the Jura devote themselves during the winter.

Oh, how I envy those who are able to pass this season by regular occupations! If I had, like them, the materials, the tools, and the skill required to create those pretty toys from wood which are typically made in the Bernese Oberland, and sold far and wide, even in Paris; or if I were but seated at a workman's bench, like the watchmakers of the Chaux-de-Fonds, or the valley of the Lac-de-Joux, who make watches so esteemed for their regularity! If I had only enough wood to make vine props, coarse pails, and barrels, like other inhabitants of the mountains, I should not complain about my lot. There is scarcely any situation in life that an assiduous attendance to labor cannot render pleasant, or at least endurable.

When we have the light, either of the lamp or the fire, I try to make beehives of straw; but although my work is very coarse, I cannot do without light; I am obliged therefore to discontinue it during a great part of the day, and I am then glad to find a means of amusement, always varying, in my grandfather's conversation. If silence and solitude were added to darkness, our situation would be indeed dreadful.

December 23rd —

Grandpapa complains of pain and numbness in all his limbs. We are compelled to walk, for some time everyday, up and down our prison as far as our limited space will allow. This exercise is necessary to us, my grandfather takes it by leaning on my arm. Today he has held his bare feet to the fire, and I remarked with grief that there was an appearance of swelling. He assures me that it is nothing new, and ought not to alarm me.

I persuade him every night to take a small quantity of wine to support his strength; and he is desirous of taking care of his health, much more to save me from anxiety than from any attachment to life. O God, preserve to me the only friend that perhaps I have remaining upon earth!

December 24th —

We invent everyday some new method of filling up our time to drive away ennui, and certainly we have gained something today, thanks to our perseverance.

"We are blind during part of the day," said my grandfather; "but the blind often know how to employ their hands and execute works whose perfection surprises us. Let us try to imitate them. Can we not plait straw in the dark? We might succeed by paying attention to it, and practice will make it easy."

We, therefore, made a first attempt; and when we had examined the result by the light of the lamp, we were not much dissatisfied with it. I think that in a few days we might arrive at the art of plaiting with some neatness.

I am going to attempt to make a straw hat, the kind that I have seen made by some young shepherds. If I succeed, I shall be the more surprised, as this work is not so simple. It requires that the strips of straw should be nicely interwoven, fastened together with numberless threads which require frequent knots, and the whole set up on a mold-like that which is used by the manufacturers of felt hats. My first attempt, I dare say, will be a very queer sort of affair.

December 25th, Christmas Day —

We have consecrated this day to prayer and meditation. To feel the full value of all that the Redeemer has done for men, a man ought to suffer misfortune. Before his time, how bitterly affliction must have been felt! How easily it must have led to discontent, and even to despair! He came upon earth, and consolation came with him. He has given us not only the wisest lessons, but also the most salutary example. Here we are, exiles in a desert; but was not our Savior conveyed to a mountain to be tempted by the devil? We have a shelter and a bed, but he had not where to lay his head. We may perhaps be forgotten of men: Jesus was cursed and persecuted by them.

These are not my own reflections, they are my grandfather's. He has given me many others which I wish that I could never forget. I was much affected by the way in which he recalled to my recollection, out of the Gospels, the birth, death, and life of Jesus. He has related to me a great number of his parables, and many of his dis courses, all full of Divine love. Our châlet seems to me like a place of worship during these recitals, with which he intermingles useful comments, applicable to our present circumstances.

Yet, though the bells have been ringing in all the valleys, the country people have been thronging the churches, and sacred hymns have sent their holy melody from village to village, none of their joyous sounds have ascended to us.

My dear neighbors, you know not all the happiness of thus assembling for the blessing of prayer, after having been separated and dispersed about in the labors of your worldly calling. Formerly custom, as well as the thoughtlessness of childhood, made me insensible to these blessings; now the thought of them affects me so much as to draw from me tears of impatience and regret. "As the hart panteth after the water brooks, so panteth my soul after thee, O God." But I trust, with David, that I shall go with the multitude into the house of God, with the voice of praise and thanksgiving among such as keep holy day.

When I go down from the mountain, like Moses, it seems as if I should be enabled to convey to my brethren the words and counsels of wisdom. I shall then say to them, "If you had learned, as I have, how necessary society is to every one, you would never entertain any other feelings for one another, except those of love and charity. Only banish for a time into such a solitude as this, those who will not understand these things, and who spread war and confusion amongst us; they will soon learn to feel their folly; they will know, by experience, that "it is not good for man to be alone; "they will learn to love their neighbors as themselves, without which love, life, instead of being a blessing, is a punishment sent from God.

December 26th —

This morning my grandfather has felt himself unwell, from having drank pure milk; happily he recovered sooner than I dared to hope. His wonderful patience seems to alleviate all his sufferings. He said to me calmly, "I have no anxiety, my dear child. It seems far from improbable that my life will be prolonged till the time of our deliverance. This is all I wish. If I had the happiness, before I die, to see you in the arms of your father, my departure hence would be more joyful than I can express. But even if God should be pleased to take me to himself while we are alone in this châlet, I have so good an opinion of you that I feel assured your trust in him would pre serve you from despair and even from fear."

"Of what use am I to you now? I am but an encumbrance, a burden which your filial piety alone enables you to bear. You do everything here. Since I have instructed you in the experience of things which you were ignorant of at first, it seems as if my task was done. Contemplate then, as I do, with courage the idea of a rather more speedy separation than we had looked for ward to, let us be prepared for whatever may happen; but still I bid you hope with confidence. The care you take of me, and a little extra prudence in the management of our provisions, will support my life till the spring, and I shall again behold the green leaves."

I could only reply by my tears to these affecting words. We remained silent, and it required some time for me to recover myself sufficiently to set to work in the darkness.

This evening my grandfather would not touch a drop of milk; and seeing that a part remained useless, he gave me a hint to make it into cheese, and he instructed me in this little work.

"It seems," he said, smiling, "that I am still of some use to you."

For want of rennet, we were obliged to turn the milk with a little vinegar. I then placed the curd in a mold of earthenware. Thus far all went off well; we shall see the result tomorrow.

On my part I gave my grandfather a hint of which he approved; it was to make him self a toast, and sop it in wine, as I had seen my aunt do for him sometimes when he felt weak or indisposed. We did it immediately; but what would I not have given for a little sugar to sprinkle upon the hot and smoking toast t Fortunately the wine we have discovered is greatly mellowed by age; it is a white wine of an excellent vintage. "A wine," said my grandfather, "which might be served at a prince's table."

"I only ask of God," he added, "to prolong my life till the vines begin to bud."

December 27th —

The cheese has perfectly succeeded. I have placed it on a shelf, and sprinkled it with salt. I cannot look at it without my mouth watering, and yet how happy should I have been if we had not had any spare milk! Today we have again milk enough to make another cheese. My grandfather has only tasted the potatoes which I have roasted in the ashes. This, with a little bread and wine, is all the nourishment that he takes. Alas! perhaps he is in pain; and, though he tries to conceal it, I can perceive that his strength is failing.

December 28th —

My grandfather now likes to lie in bed later, and to go earlier to rest. He considers that next to a little exercise, the comfortable warmth he obtains when lying under the wool blanket and the straw, agrees best with him. It is impossible for anyone to take greater care of himself than he does, or to do it in a less selfish manner. What ever he does, whatever he says, both instructs and affects me. When he sits in his chair, he is mostly employed in reading, and teaching me. What an immense progress I have made, under his instruction, in a few weeks! I left the plains with the feelings and notions of a child; I have become almost a man here with a rapidity at which I am astonished.

The day which has passed away has not been marked by any event. I have worked as usual, and almost the whole time in the dark. I acquire so much facility in the practice of this, that it seems as if my sight had been transferred to the ends of my fingers. I can detect the slightest error by the feeling; and this inspires me with reflections that are quite new to me. I find some thing so interesting in this way of proceeding, that I would advise even those persons to try it who are in no need of it. The sight is such a ready and obliging servant, that it does not permit us to require of our other senses all that we might obtain from them. The touch is also a faithful friend, but it waits the orders of our will to be of service to us; it leaves it to the mind both to guide and direct it. Thus each of our senses and our members retains its proper functions; the mind governs, the body obeys.

These are the reflections that our present circumstances inspire. I did not think some time ago, that I should fix my mind upon such subjects; I have learned more in thirty days of confinement, than I did in a whole life of freedom.

December 29th —

The days on which there is no event to vary our painful existence, my thoughts are more vividly fixed upon what may happen without; and the moment they fly from our dark and solitary dwelling, they settle them selves upon you, my dear father. Nevertheless, I am always perplexed where to find you. My first impulse is to seek for you in our house, or in our fields. I see you there alone and sad, your eyes often turning to the heights where we are suffering from your absence. You at least know where we are, and you cannot have given up all hopes of seeing us again. For, after all, we have not been deprived of every resource. But how are we to know what has prevented you from coming to our aid? I try in vain to flatter myself that nothing fatal has hindered you, for a sad foreboding tells me that the day of our deliverance will be one of mourning.

Why did you not remain with us? Per haps you have perished in trying to save our cattle. In the midst of the darkness which so often surrounds me, I listen with a superstitious dread. I fancy that I heard the an gels warning me of my misfortune. I think I have discovered God's secret intentions, and I can scarcely recover from this wandering of the mind. My grandfather's words at length recall me to reason and patience, and I respect the veil which conceals from me both the past and the future. *Have* I lost my father? *Shall* I lose my grandfather? Alas! I know not, and it is doubtless good for me to remain in ignorance. O God, I will no more offend thee by my anxiety and distrust! I will embrace my Savior's cross, and wait with resignation for the accomplishment of thy will.

December 30th —

The end of the year draws nigh. This is a day on which my schoolfellows enjoy a liberty that they have longed for too much; they do not go to school today, and they think it their greatest happiness. So thought I too, when I was in the village; my thoughts are much changed now. What would I not give to pass several hours a day in that schoolroom, which I used to look upon as a prison! I hear the morning bell at whose sound we assemble; we go in helter-skelter, with our books under our arms; every one takes his place; the master rises, and we rise also; prayer begins and sanctifies our labors.

Then begins the confused murmur of voices, repeating in a low tone what they will shortly be called upon to repeat aloud. The copybooks are opened, and the rustling of the leaves on all sides mingles with numberless sounds, which the master interrupts by striking upon his desk with his large beechen ruler. Several of the boys smile slily at one another.

He is going to dictate the exercise; all pens are prepared, and run-over the paper together. Then comes the practice of arithmetic, reading, and singing.

Thus passing from one work to another, in a society formed only with the view of interesting and pleasing them, the boys, nevertheless, are constantly casting impatient glances at the wooden clock. The quiet pendulum continues its steady pace, the weights imperceptibly descend, and the schoolboy every moment marks their descent upon the wall. Three hours have at length passed slowly away; the time of breaking up has come.

Scarcely is the class dismissed than joyous cries and the noise of rushing out are heard, instead of the former silence and restraint. They spring forward, they run, they jostle one another; games are formed in front of the school—too often mingled with quarrels.

I too have had my part in these labors and these pleasures; it seems as if I partook of them still in their remembrance here. It is a waking dream—I remember and I forget . . .

"Poor Louis!" said my grandfather, "what new cause have you got for sighing? Shall I be obligated to forbid you the relaxation which I recommended to you myself? Have more command over your thoughts as well as your pen; occupy both with matter that will serve to strengthen your mind; consider that your present condition requires the greatest firmness, and soon perhaps may require even more."

"Are you not so well tonight, dear grandfather?"

"Yes, my child, I am much as usual; and if I have just lain down, it is only for prudence' sake. I wish to manage so well that in two or three months we may go gaily together down the mountain with Blanchette running before us. They will be so glad to see us!"

"They will not wait till we set out, I can assure you; and they will come and knock at our door sooner than you think for."

"They will come and knock at our door!" In repeating my words my grandfather looked grave and pressed my hand.

"And if the messenger of liberty should come and summon me, not to our village, but to heaven, what would you do, my boy? Let us see. We ought to foresee and prepare ourselves for such an event. You will be, I doubt not, an excellent nurse; and as long as I live I shall rely upon your strength of mind; but afterwards . . . you will have other duties . . . to my remains; shall you be able to fulfill them?"

I interrupted my grandfather by my sobs; I begged of him not to go on. We remained some time embracing each other; and now, having added this painful scene to my journal, I will try and forget it in sleep.

December 31st —

Happy day! my grandfather has more appetite and more strength; he has taken a little coffee with milk, he has eaten more than usual, and has refreshed himself with a drop of wine. Thus, that which is a poison when taken improperly, or in excess, as many persons are in the habit of doing, in this case is a medicine whose effects I have good reason to bless.

The last day of the year has passed well. Grant, O God, for Christ's sake, that I may be thankful for it, and finish it in adoring thy power and goodness!

January 1st —

Last year, on this day, I was in the midst of my family. The evening before, my father went into town to make some little purchases, of which I had my share. In the morning I went with him to church; we had some relations to dinner; the children danced and sang, and kept up the feast to a late hour.

If I had been asked by somebody some months ago to guess where I should spend New Year's Day this year, I would certainly not have ever imagined the predicament that I now suffer and see around me. Unexpected events happen so often to men that they ought to be constantly upon their guard, like a soldier who is keeping watch in the neighborhood of an enemy.

My grandfather, thinking that this would be but a sorrowful day for me, has been doing all he can to amuse me; he has been trying to teach me some games which are not without instruction; he has proposed questions to me, which admit of being solved in a humorous manner; his conversation has been more gay and cheerful than usual, and we made a sort of feast at our supper. He made me add the first cheese I had made to our roasted potatoes, and I found it quite as nice as I expected. I did not even refuse to have his toast. It was truly a feast for such hermits as we are.

Nor was the poor goat forgotten. I looked out the best hay for her, gave her fresh straw, a double ration of salt, and a three fold allowance of kisses.

May the Lord, whom we have invoked both morning and evening, preserve the grandson to his grandfather, and the grandfather to his grandchild!

My grandfather has requested that he might add here a few words with his own hand.

In the name of God, Amen —

It may happen that I be taken away from my friends, before I have the power of making my last wishes known —

I have no general disposition to make with respect to my worldly goods; but I wish to express my sense of the care and devotion of my dear grandson, Louis Lopraz, now present; and as it is out of my power to make him the least present on this day, I beg my heirs to supply the defect, by giving him on my behalf,

- my repeating watch;
- my carbine;
- my Bible, (which was my father's also); and lastly, my steel seal, on which are engraved my initials, which are the same as those of my godchild and grandson —

These trifling tokens of remembrance will be most precious to him, I am convinced, on account of the affection which unites us; a bond which death itself will not dissolve.

Such is my will

Louis Lopraz

January 1, 1826

At the Chalet d'Azinder

Dear and venerable parent! let me in my turn record in my journal the deep expression of my gratitude. I feel what an inestimable blessing it has been for me to have lived with you in this lonely retreat. I wanted no reward, beyond the kind testimony which you have been good enough to give of me; and that surely ought to suffice. May you yet, for a long time, enjoy the society of our friends and relations! With this devout wish, in which they are all so much interested, I begin the new year.

January 2nd —

For some time we have not heard a sound from outside, and our seclusion has been the more complete. We conclude from this that a great deal more snow has fallen, and that probably the châlet is buried entirely under its mass. However the iron tube rises still above it, and the smoke escapes freely; today some flakes of snow have fallen through this narrow passage.

These white messengers of winter are the only connection we have with the world beyond our den.

If our clock were to stop, we should have no means of knowing how the time passes. The only means we should have of discerning the night from the day is by the glimmering of light which we can perceive in the morning through the funnel.

As a consolation, we suffer very little cold in our silent cavern. We might have more reason to fear that our dwelling would become unwholesome; but the little current of air which passes through the chimney is sufficient to purify the place by yielding us a fresh supply of cold, crisp mountain air.

When we have lighted the lamp, and, employed in our daily occupations, we sit before a clear fire, we sometimes forget our misfortune, and regain some little degree of cheerfulness. At such moments, I am sure that our situation would excite the envy of some of my companions. Have we not all, at times, wished to be Robinson Crusoe on his desert island? Nevertheless, the barrier of the ocean which separated him from other men, was one far more difficult to overcome than our isolation. He had no hope but in the arrival of some ship driven off her course, but we are assured that the snow will be thawed sooner or later. May God only be pleased to preserve our lives till then!

January 4th —

It was impossible for me to resume my pen last night; or rather I did not think of it. Alas! I had far different matters to attend to.

The day had passed tranquilly. My grandfather had little appetite, but he did not complain of anything. In the evening, after supper, as he was sitting by the fireside, enjoying with me this moment, which is always the pleasantest of the day, he suddenly turned pale, sank down, and but for my assistance, would have fallen into the fire.

I shrieked with alarm; I caught him in my arms, and with a strength which I could never have supposed that I possessed, I carried him to his bed, where I first set him down, and then laid him at full length. His head and his hands were quite cold; the blood had flowed back to the heart, and I was very careful not to raise his head by placing anything under it. I recollected, at the moment, some instructions which he had given me some days before, in case of such accidents. I kept his head low, and the blood was not long in returning to it; his senses returned at the same moment.

"Where am I? What! upon my bed?" said my grandfather.

"Certainly Grandpapa," I replied. "You have been feeling a little faint, and I thought it better to place you here; and you perceive that I did right, for the moment you were laid down you recovered your senses."

"He has carried me here! God be praised, your strength, dear child, increases in the same proportion as mine diminishes. In short we lose nothing, as you see; we find, on the contrary, in this natural revolution, new reasons, on your part, for exertion; on mine, for affection towards you."

He then threw his arms round my neck; I knelt down by the bed, and we remained thus for a good while.

"Do not alarm yourself at what has happened," he said calmly, after some minutes. "I attribute it to the fancy I had to taste some of your goat's-milk cheese. I ought to have foreseen that, since milk disagrees with me, the cheese would be much more improper. The crisis is past, and I feel inclined to sleep. This disposition to sleep is as pleasant as the feelings which preceded the fainting fit were painful."

He soon fell asleep; I watched some time by him, and when I saw that he was quite comfortable, I blessed God, and in my turn lay down, commending myself to his protection.

Today I have been occupied with house hold business. My grandfather remarked that our linen, stockings, and the flannel which he wears next his skin, required washing; and I therefore begged him to remain in bed. I then made some lye, that is, as well as it could be made without soap. He directed my operations. A tolerably large cloth, which serves us for a table-cloth, enabled me to separate the ashes from the things that were to be washed. A pail did the duty of a washing-tub. I then put all these things into hot water; in the evening they were all ready for drying. I am going to leave them hanging round the fire till the morning. Some embers which remain, the warmth from the hearth, and the current of air from the chimney, will complete this important operation.

I forgot to say, that having observed my grandfather rubbing his body and his limbs, I begged him to avail himself of my feeble assistance even for that. I rubbed him well with a part of the blanket that we had devoted to this work, for nearly an hour. He is convinced that nothing is better to make the blood circulate, to supply the place of the exercise which he can no longer take, and of the open air, from which we have been so long obliged to refrain.

Alas! I found his poor body in a sad state of emaciation. While rendering him this trifling care, he never ceased thanking me. "It seems to me," he said, "as if you were restoring me to life; I feel a comfortable warmth renewed in my limbs; and I breathe more freely."

These words inspired me with fresh ardor; and as he appeared distressed by the trouble I was taking, "Do you not observe," I asked, "that I am myself taking wholesome exercise? I assure you that, in being of service to you, I am doing myself good; and I beg you will often make use of a remedy which is so salutary to your physician." Grandfather is reposing tranquilly near me; however, I have made ample amends for my silence yesterday evening, by writing the history of two days.

January 5th —

My grandfather spoke to me this morning of his state, without concealing anything from me. All his words sound still in my ears. What gentleness and wisdom combined! I should be inexcusable if I did not profit by them, even young as I am.

"My child," he said, after desiring me to sit down at the head of his bed; "I can no longer conceal it from you; the end of my life is not far distant. Can we keep my soul in my body long enough for me to behold the day of thy deliverance? I know not; but I dare not indulge the least hope of it; my debility increases with astonishing rapidity, and it is probable that I shall leave you alone to complete our sad winter.

"You will, I doubt not, be more afflicted by our separation, than disturbed by your own desolation, and your grief will be greater than your fears; but I rely too firmly upon your courage and piety to believe that you will suffer yourself to be completely cast down. You will remember your father, whom, I trust, you will certainly see again; and that thought will support you. You will soon be convinced that the dangers you run in this châlet will not be increased by my death. On the contrary, I have become a hindrance; you will no longer be in dread of want; and perhaps at the moment of leaving the mountain you will have less encumbrance. I beg you only to have patience. Do not expose yourself too soon. In so long a captivity a day or two more or less is nothing, and you will risk everything by anticipating the favorable moment.

"And why should you hurry yourself? Your health up to this time has not suffered by our seclusion. You will no longer, it is true, have our conversations to amuse you; but how many prisoners are condemned to silence for many long years! These, again, often have a conscience stung with remorse; while you will be sustained by the consoling recollection of duties fulfilled. Only one thing causes me much anxiety, my dear Louis, if I must tell it you; I fear the effect that my death may have upon your imagination. When you see this body deprived of life, it will cause you a feeling of dread, perhaps of horror, very unreasonable indeed, but which many people cannot overcome.

"But why should you be afraid of the remains of your old grandfather? Are you afraid of me when I am asleep? The other night when I fainted you had no idea that I could hurt you, you only perceived the necessity of assisting me, and you did your duty like a brave man. Well! if you see me fall into that last swoon which is called death, conduct yourself in the same sensible manner. My passing will then only require from you one last obligation, whenever nature shall inform you that my hour has come. You will have sufficient strength for it, which you proved the other night when you carried me to this bed.

"You see that door; it leads into the dairy, where we never enter, because it is useless to us; there you will dig a grave as deep as you can to deposit my body, till the time when you can remove it, and give it, in the spring, a regular burial in the village churchyard.

"When these sad duties are ended, you will find yourself very lonely in this place; you will shed many tears; you will call to me often, but I shall make you no answer. Do not give way to useless regret; address yourself only to Him, who always answers when we call upon him with faith. You will understand better than ever the power of his aid; everything else may fail you, but He will supply the place of all."

Such were the exhortations which my grandfather addressed to me this morning; and as he found himself comforted by having given them to me, he appeared more calm, more serene, and almost joyful. For myself, I cannot be persuaded that a spirit so free and so firm can inhabit a body which is near its dissolution. The danger is before my eyes, and yet it seems far distant. May God confirm these presages of good!

January 6th —

Another day is gone! These are our words every night. My impatience increases, and I think the spring will never come. Is it the fear of being alone, against which my grandfather cautioned me, that causes me so much anxiety? I seek to divest myself of such unworthy feelings; I will think no more of myself, but of the love and mercy of God my Savior, of his favor. Ah! if I now pray for my grandfather's recovery, it is no longer for my own sake, nor to spare me the horrors of solitude.

January 7th —

Darkness is particularly irksome to the sick, they even say that it is injurious to persons in good health. Light was made for man, and man for the light. We have contrived this morning a way to save our oil without remaining entirely in the dark. I have made a sort of night lamp with a thin slice of cork, in which I have fixed a slender wick. This feeble light is sufficient for me to work by; it enlivens my grandfather a little; we shall make use of it for the future, and we shall only light the lamp when we absolutely want it, for I find it altogether impossible to write without it.

Doubtless, persons accustomed to the light of the humblest dwelling in our village would think our châlet very gloomy; but after the darkness in which we have lived so long, it is a pleasure to us to get a glimpse of one another, to go about without being obliged to feel our way, and to be able to distinguish by this pale light our day from our night.

A layer of oil swims in a glass three-fourths full of water, and our little sun floats upon this oil. It is placed upon the table, and we are just able to discern by its light the different articles which serve to furnish our kitchen. This half daylight, about the same brightness as that of the early day break, leads to reflection, and at the same time makes us a little more cheerful; it reminds us of churches in which a lighted lamp invites to prayer. None of my grandfather's actions escape me; I see him often clasp his hands, and raise his eyes, or fix them upon me. Ah! I then guess his thoughts, and without speaking we join in the same wish and the same prayer.

January 10th —

My God, thy will be done! . . . . I am now alone with thee, far away from all the world. The day before yesterday I cannot go on; I cannot yet relate the circumstances of his death. My paper is drenched with my tears.

January 12th —

Yes, it is the 12th of January today; two days have gone by since I wrote the above lines My senses are recovering, and if it please God will yet gain strength. If I did not feel that the Lord is with me and about my path, I think I should die too, were it only through fear.

January 13th and 14th —

I had gone to bed on the 7th full of hope, my grandfather seemed to me better than usual; but before I had fallen asleep I heard him groan, and I leaped out of bed. Without waiting for him to call me I dressed myself, lighted the night lamp, which was prepared, and asked the him what he was suffering.

"A faintness . . .," he said; "like the other day, or perhaps . . ."

There he stopped.

"Will you take a drop of wine, dear grandfather?"

"No, my child; only bathe my temples and rub my hands with a little vinegar . . . and . . . take the *Imitation of Jesus Christ*. Read, dear child, that place which you know . . . where I have placed a mark."

I obeyed, and when I had rubbed his hands and temples with the vinegar, I light ed the lamp that I might see better; I knelt down, and with a trembling voice I read the page he had marked.

It was at the commencement of the ninth chapter of the fourth book. "Lord! all that the heavens and the earth contain are thine. I will present unto thee a willing offering, and will abide with thee forever;" as far as these words, "I present to thee also all that is good within me, that it may please thee to correct and sanctify it, to accept and to perfect it more and more, and lead me to a good and blessed end, although worthless and unprofitable, and the least of all men."

When I had read thus far he stopped me, told me to draw near, took my hands in his, and offered up a prayer which I will faithfully write down as far as my memory will allow.

"Lord! at the moment when I am about to appear before thee I ought to be occupied with nothing but my own salvation, and to tremble at the thoughts of thy judgments; pardon me if I cannot remove my thoughts from another subject which disturbs me. Thou art about to take me to thyself, and I must leave this poor child alone. After having separated him from his father, I am about to abandon him myself!"

"I tremble at the thoughts of what he is about to suffer; I fear, above all, lest his faith should grow weak, and that he should want confidence in thee. Thou hearest, O Lord: listen to me I beseech thee! Let my example instruct him, and by seeing me depart in peace let him learn to live as I hope to die, trusting wholly in the Lord Jesus Christ!"

"Alas! I had desired to leave the mountain with him, and to behold again our forests and orchards, but thy will has otherwise ordained; suffer then my grandchild, at least, to revisit them. Inspire him with sufficient firmness and prudence. Grant that, after my death, he may be as he has ever been during my life, attentive, persevering, and full of courage. Let not his father or our friends have to reproach me with having brought him here."

"If it should be thy pleasure to restore him to them, I have but to bless my lot; for I feel sensible that the trial to which thou hast subjected him, through me, will be of lasting service to him; he will never forget the impressions he has received in this place."

"Pardon me, O Lord! that I occupy my thoughts so much with him; it is thy glory that I still seek in the midst of these sufferings, and I am more anxious about the eternal salvation of my dear boy than about the dangers that may threaten his life."

Such were nearly his words. He pronounced them slowly with a weak voice, and only by long intervals. Then he made me recite all the prayers I knew by heart; he recollected himself, occasionally, passages from the Bible, and sayings of our Savior, and repeated them with a fervor and resignation which made me weep.

I must add one circumstance, trifling in deed, but which affected me still more deeply. Blanchette, surprised perhaps at seeing the light burning at such an unusual hour, began to bleat violently.

"Poor Blanchette!" said the dying man; "I must take my last leave of you. Go and loose her, child, and bring her up to the bed."

I did what he desired, and Blanchette in her usual familiar way placed her two fore feet on the edge of the bed, to see if she could find something to eat. We had accustomed her to take a little salt out of our hands. I thought I should please Grandpapa by placing a little in his hand; Blanchette did not fail to run to it, and to lick it a long time.

"Continue to be a good nurse," he said, placing his hand with some difficulty on her neck. He then turned away his hand, and I led Blanchette back to her manger and tied her up.

My dying Grandpapa from that time scarcely uttered any complete thoughts, he only gave me to understand that he wished me to remain near him holding his hand; I felt at intervals a slight pressure, and as his looks spoke to me at the same moment, I understood that he was trying to collect his last strength to express his affection for me, and to tell me that his love for me would only cease with his life.

I spoke some words of affection to him; then his countenance lighted up, and I saw that it would be a pleasure to him if I went on. I leaned, therefore, towards him, and said, with all the firmness I could assume, "Adieu! adieu! we shall meet again in heaven. I will strive to be faithful to the lessons you have given me, in order to obtain that great reward. I believe in God, our Father; I believe in the merits of the Savior, and the grace of the Holy Spirit. Be not uneasy on my account; you have done so much to instruct me, that God is now all I want and all my desire."

Here the pressure of the hand was more distinct; and after making a vain effort to answer me, he could only express the pleasure he felt by a sigh.

"I will remember," I continued, "all the advice you have given me for my preservation. For the love of you, I will neglect no thing which may tend to prolong my life, and procure my deliverance from this châlet. Adieu! dear grandfather! Alas! you will meet my mother in heaven, and, perhaps, my father too; tell them I will strive at all times to follow their example and yours. Adieu! adieu!"

I felt another very faint pressure; it was the last. His hand, which had been growing gradually cold, let mine drop; he died without a struggle, without even a sigh.

I was not horror struck at first; I was too much stunned. But when I had recovered from the first shock, and found myself alone in this wild desolate place—alone with a corpse, I then felt an involuntary shuddering, especially when night was come.

In the morning, I recollected myself sufficiently to wind up the clock, and to milk Blanchette. The cold obliged me to light a fire; that engaged me for some time: but then I fell into a deep stupefaction. It happened that there arose, in the evening, so violent a wind as to cause me to hear those mournful sounds of moaning to which I had been for some time unaccustomed.

I was by the fireside; I was watching by the light of the night lamp, with my back turned to the bed. Gradually a fit of shivering came over me; I could no longer command my thoughts; my distress would have gone on increasing, and perhaps have proved fatal, if I had not thought of a means of calming it down, which one might have suppose only adapted to increase it. I went up to the body, at first with reluctance, after wards with more resolution; I looked at it, I even dared to touch it. It was a painful moment; however, I persevered; I repeated the action several times, and I felt my terrors gradually subside.

From that moment I did not cease, from time to time, to return to the side of the corpse; I fulfilled those offices which persons who are accustomed to them perform with so much coolness. The expression of the countenance was so calm and so mild that it again drew from me a flood of tears.

"No," I replied, sobbing, "the mortal remains of my dear old grandfather no longer disturb me."

However, my anguish returned, when I began to feel sleepy. "Shall I go," I thought, "down by the corpse?" I had not the resolve for that, I must confess; and I sought a miserable resource against the superstitious fears which were beginning again to plague me. I went and took refuge with Blanchette. The warmth and feeling of life which the contact of this poor animal gave me, the gentle sound of her ruminating, restored to me some degree of courage.

But why, when the light was put out, did I begin to tremble again? Poor child that I am! what safety could I find in that faint light? My breath extinguishes it; my hand lights it again; and yet I depend upon that glimmering flame for tranquility.

At length the Almighty, to whom I prayed fervently, had compassion upon me; he restored me to composure, and granted that I slept soundly through the remaining night.

The next day, as soon as I awoke, the conflicts of the former night began again; I busied myself as much as possible with my goat and my work, and more particularly I frequently approached the corpse; I even held for a time that dear and venerable head in my arms. The more my fears subsided, the more my affliction increased; and I gave myself credit for so natural and reasonable a change.

I began then to think what I ought to do about the burial, and I called to mind what my grandfather had said to me. I was terribly alarmed by the difficulties that presented themselves. Besides, my grandfather had spoken to me of the danger of premature interment; and I believe he did so with a secret view to this emergency. I resolved therefore to wait till nature itself should compel me to fulfill this last duty. The strong affection which I had for my grandfather prevented me from yielding to the unworthy motive of removing from my sight, as soon as possible, a repulsive object.

Bed-time was almost as painful to me as it was the night before. In order to acquire a little more firmness, I thought of taking a small quantity of the wine which had been too sparingly rationed by my grandfather.

When I had poured into his glass what appeared to be sufficient, I was seized, before I carried it to my lips, with a most painful oppression of the heart. "Useless aid," I chastened myself; but then I thought of the pleasure which accompanied my dear grandfather's first sip. Being unaccustomed to any kind of fermented liquor, and my exhaustion after so many trials, caused the wine to take a powerful effect, and I had another good night.

I tried to write in my journal on the 10th, but I found it impossible to do so; however, on that day from the morning, I was in a much more comfortable state of mind. Prayer had given me courage; my feelings became calm by degrees; and, as my grandfather had foretold, fear yielded to sorrow.

How many tears I shed over your body, my venerable parent! I see, however, that death is beginning to leave its livid traces. My senses would have revolted at the sight, had my heart been less full. It was in vain that I was warned that it was become a case of necessity to prepare for the burial; I thought of the means of still preserving those decaying remains. At length I thought of God's will so strongly expressed in Scripture, and which is in such strict accordance with reason and nature: "Then shall the dust return to the earth as it was."

I collected my tools, and opened the door of the dairy. "Thus," I thought to myself, "you pass through different labors! After having been both nurse and physician, you are now the gravedigger; you are compelled to perform yourself that office which relations have a repugnance to witnessing."

The first strokes revolted me; I was obliged to pause. It was not that my arms refused their office; it was the distress of my mind that deprived me of the energy that was requisite. Every time that I smote the earth, a loud echo answered from the vaulted roof, which was built over like a cellar. I was obliged to get accustomed to this work, and I devoted the whole day to a labor that might have been accomplished in two hours.

In fact, the soil was light and sandy, and at length I was able to shovel it out, without being obliged to dig it first with the spade. I availed myself of this facility to dig a very deep pit; for, I thought to myself, if the châlet should be unoccupied for some time, whether I leave it, or whether I die in my turn, I ought to do all I can to protect the body from beasts of prey. Besides, my health required the grave to be very deep, so that no smell should exhale from the place where it was made. I went on then with my mournful work, until the pit was over my head.

The clock struck six. The night was come, and dark thoughts came with it. For, even without being able to perceive any external objects, the very idea that darkness reigned around, made me feel, even in the châlet, the sad impressions of night. I had not the courage to complete the interment, though it was becoming absolutely necessary.

This violent exercise I had taken soon sent me to sleep. It was only delayed a few moments by the caresses of Blanchette, who seems well pleased to have me so near her, and who does not object to serve me for a pillow.

On the 11th of January, my first thought was to complete my painful task; and when I had lighted my lamp, I again found my courage fail. I was obliged to have recourse again to means which I ought to have known how to avoid. Instead of breakfasting as usual upon warm milk and potatoes, I took a little bread and wine. This nourishment restored to me some degree of firmness, which was not enough to do honor to my character, but of which I availed myself without delay. I had reflected beforehand upon the means of executing the task, and I had prepared everything the evening before. I placed on two stools, by the side of the bed, a plank which was sufficiently large both in breadth and length, in fact the very one whose fall was the cause of my discovering the *Imitation of Jesus Christ*. I then got upon the bed, and putting a cord under the armpits of the corpse, I succeeded in bringing this extremity of the body on the plank. The lower part gave me less trouble. I tied the body on the plank, and when I saw it thus, with the hands crossed upon the breast, yielding to my will, with the head inclining mournfully to one side, I burst into tears and uttered loud cries.

"My grandfather! you are leaving me; you hear me no more; you cannot answer me!"

I know not what unmeaning words I thus addressed to this dead body, in the transports of my grief. It would have lasted perhaps a long time, if I had had a comforter near me; his words, perhaps, would only have irritated and inflamed my grief. But when I saw these cold remains as insensible to my complaints as to my actions, its motionless appearance soon restored to me the serenity of which I stood in so much need.

I had prepared two rollers of wood; I placed them in a proper position, and with drawing with the greatest precaution the stool which supported the lower extremity of the body, I let the end of the plank gently down upon the ground. In spite of all my efforts, the operation was not so successful at the other end, and the fall of the body was so sudden as to give me a beating at the heart, which compelled me again to stop.

Dear grandfather, when you taught me, at the front of our house, to convey a heavy body upon rollers, we little thought that I should ever have occasion to profit by your lessons on so sad an occasion. The recollection of what you then said to me recurred vividly to my imagination; I thought I heard you again; and when the motion of this funeral burden shook your head, as if it were making signs of approval, I was so much affected, that I turned away my eyes, as persons walking along a precipice do through fear of giddiness.

I had smoothed and leveled the way; the corpse was soon at the side of the grave. It would have been easy for me to let it fall in; but I could not bear to treat it with so little respect. Two smaller planks placed across supported it above the grave. "When that which bore the feet was once removed, it was placed in an oblique position, after having experienced another shock which I could not prevent; a cord which I passed under the shoulders, after having fixed one of the ends firmly to a stake, allowed me to let the body descend gently into its place of rest.

All the difficulties were now surmounted, what remained to be done gave me no anxiety with respect to the execution of it; I could now freely give way to my grief. Seated upon the mound which I had raised with my hands, I wept a long time by the open grave. I could not summon resolution to throw the first shovelful of earth upon the body.

"Before I fulfill this dreadful duty," I said to myself, "let me in the best way I can dis charge that of a priest." I kneeled down immediately, and searched my memory for all I knew of prayers and scriptural passages adapted to this ceremony. I took the *Imitation of Jesus Christ* in my hand, and knowing it so well, it was not difficult to me to find out places such as were applicable to the occasion, and which my grandfather had pointed out to me.

O my dear grandfather, you are now happy! I alone at this time stand in need of consolation; it was with a joy beyond expression that I read over your mortal remains the chapter upon "the quiet and peaceful man," and that "on purity of heart and sincerity of intention." There were so many features like yours, that it seemed to me as if the author had been drawing your portrait.

"Begin," says he, "by establishing peace firmly in yourself, and you may then be able to communicate it to others."

That is what you have done, good and just man! and your peace of mind is bequeathed to me.

"The peaceful man confers more benefits upon his neighbor than the learned man," says the *Imitation*. I cannot conceive, dear parent, what was wanting in your knowledge, though you have a hundred times spoken of your ignorance; but you were so kind and gentle, that you inspired me with an ardent desire to testify my love to you by my docility, and to show my docility by the progress I made.

"If you are good and pure," so speaks the book, "you will see clearly, and under stand everything; a pure heart penetrates earth and heaven. Every man judges of external things by the disposition of his heart."

You were good and pure, my dear grandfather! which enabled you to read my heart more easily and more clearly than I could myself. You must often have found me deserving of reproof, and nevertheless your indulgence was greater than your penetration. Your knowledge of me, in this respect, was useless; you did not cease, with all my faults, to love me.

These were some of the words which I addressed to him with tenderness. It seemed as if, in speaking aloud, I was no longer in solitude. The book replied to me, and kept up my emotion. At length I stopped from exhaustion; I recovered myself, and no longer delayed doing what remained to be done. The grave was soon filled. I passed the remainder of the day by engraving with the point of my knife the following inscription upon a piece of maple:—

HERE RESTS THE BODY OF LOUIS LOPRAZ
WHO DIED IN THE NIGHT OF JANUARY THE 7TH 1826,
IN THE ARMS OF HIS GRANDSON, LOUIS LOPRAZ,
WHO BURIED HIM WITH HIS OWN HANDS

I nailed this piece of wood to a post, which I fixed upon the mound over the grave; after which I shut the door and returned to the kitchen, where Blanchette was my only companion.

However, although I was much more at my ease now the corpse was no longer lying on the bed, I found that I had not quite overcome my weakness. I resolved to struggle with it. I had been led by it to lock the door of the dairy; I went immediately, opened it, and then fastened it only with the latch. I determined also to pay frequent visits to the tomb, and always without a light; I have done this for two days, and I say my prayers there night and morning.

The day before yesterday seemed wearisome and to want occupation. The urgent business in which I had till then been employed no longer called forth my exertions, and I had now to contend with myself. I sought in labor amusement which I could not find. I endeavored to fix my thoughts upon everything which I wanted to do; but I could not escape from myself. In the evening I tried to write, but again I was unable to do it.

Yesterday, which was the 13th, a thought came into my head to read over my journal from the beginning. It will easily be believed that this reading affected me greatly; but I ought also to add, that it did me much good in recalling to me, with renewed force, the lessons and the virtues of my grandfather. As soon as I had finished, I felt the want of pouring out my grief in this journal, which I began by his advice. At length I devoted the whole of yesterday and today to the relating of the sad event which has caused such a melancholy change in my situation.

January 15th —

Yes, my lot is greatly changed! I perceive it more and more everyday. What then? When I had a friend with me, I dared to complain! I compared my present situation with my former one. How much I now regret the condition I then deplored! God punishes me for my discontent. I am alone! I am alone! That thought pursues me all day.

January 16th —

I passed the day in the same state; I felt myself depressed and discouraged, and I should have gone to bed as desolate as I did the night before, but for one circumstance, which I cannot call a miracle because it was only a natural occurrence, but which struck me as a warning of Providence.

I had concluded my silent evening; I had just put out the fire, and was going to do the same with the light, when I heard a slight noise in the chimney. It was a bit of rubbish which had fallen covered with soot. The soot had caught fire and caused a faint smell, and I went under the flue to see that all was safe. While with my head thrown back I was vainly searching for any traces of fire on the walls, a star passed over the iron tube, and I observed it crossing it slowly at its greatest breadth.

This appearance lasted but a moment, yet it was enough to affect me greatly.

One of those suns, then, which the Creator has dispersed over the firmament, sends its rays to shine upon me, and visits me even at the bottom of my tomb; it speaks to me of the power of my God; it invites me to adore him and to hope! I could not resist this appeal, I fell on my knees, and for the first time for many days I felt again my soul burn with that ardor which the lessons of my grandfather had kindled in it.

January 17th —

How difficult it is to preserve and entertain the salutary impressions which a good impulse has produced in us! I had gone to bed full of joy, and I rose up more languid than ever. I recollected, as nearly as I could, the hour when the star passed by, and I hoped to see it again today; but whether it changed its position, or whether the sky was clouded, I know not, but I could not perceive it.

January 18th —

While my soul is vainly seeking the nourishment it has lost, my body is well sup plied with food, which, if it cannot make my heart glad, ought at least to give me con fidence. The portion of Blanchette's milk which I do not consume serves me everyday to make a small cheese; I do this much less by precaution than to direct my thoughts. But I do not get accustomed to my solitude; I try in vain to invite sleep, and to remain at rest. The days seem to have no end.

January 19th —

I write for writing sake. "What can I find to fill my journal? If it were to give a true picture, it would be one of the most frightful sorrow. I try to take up my pen, as formerly, and to exercise my mind a little; useless endeavor! I cannot shake off this torpor.

January 20th —

The malady I am suffering from is the worst that I can imagine. My first grief when we found ourselves imprisoned, my fear when the wolves seemed to be attacking us, the mournful scene of my grandfather's death and burial, never made me suffer so much as the depression which I now feel. Is it a weariness of mind which oppresses me? I never knew the torment of this feeling from which even prayer cannot release me.

January 21st —

As long as the poor goat has a hand to feed her she will never trouble herself about the void that surrounds her. I am the same to her as my grandfather would have been, or as a stranger would be. She stands in need of me without being conscious of it; she avails herself of my care without acknowledging it; I am sometimes almost tempted to reproach her. What folly! Ingratitude cannot dwell with brutes who are without reason. But I myself, enlightened as I am by the Divine intelligence, do I know how to make that use of it for which God gave it to me? Am I more grateful than this poor ignorant brute? Unhappy being that I am, may I only have grace to preserve myself from murmuring and despair!

January 22nd —

I write down this date in my book; there is nothing else to make me remember the day. What am I become!

January 23rd —

I have been near perishing by a sudden terrible death, which would have surprised me in the midst of my sinful despondency. May I again call this a miracle? What good would it be to me to know how God deals with me, provided the events which he directs produce their proper effect?

I had remarked for some days that the weather was much milder; I scarcely wanted any fire, and the smoke ascended less easily. Today, about two o'clock in the afternoon, I heard a dull rumbling sound like the distant rolling of thunder; it seemed to approach rapidly, it soon became fearful, and I felt a violent shock.

I uttered a loud cry. Several utensils were thrown down, a thick cloud of dust filled the kitchen, the cracking of the beams told me that the châlet had been severely shaken; however, I saw everything was right as far as I could see.

I made the round of the other parts of the house. I had scarcely entered the cow-house when I saw the fearful traces of the accident; the earth was covered with plaster, the wall had given way; it was visibly out of the perpendicular, but it had not fallen; a part of the roof towards the mountain was broken. This was all; and I concluded that the mass which had caused the damage had fallen against the châlet. Was it a piece of rock detached from the precipice that over hangs it? Was it not more probably an avalanche which had been formed a little above, in consequence of the mildness of the weather, and which having not yet acquired sufficient strength and size, had been unable to overleap the obstacle opposed to it.

My emotion was very great; it even lasts yet; I frequently thank the Almighty for the warning he has given me. May it arouse my heart up, and may it not sink again! Yes; I confess that this new trial was necessary for me. I had fallen into a guilty state of dejection; I am happily delivered from it, and I will go and bless God upon my grandfather's tomb.

January 24th —

God is not willing that I should be again exposed to needless dejection; he has inflicted upon me a new subject of anxiety; my goat's milk decreases. I thought I had observed it for some days; it is now no longer doubtful.

The Journal of a Young Man of Jura

January 25th —

My grandfather certainly had foreseen my being detained here for some significant period after his passing, for he gave me much advice how to act in order to extricate myself from deprivation and embarrassment. He asked me one day, "Have you given any thought to what must be done if Blanchette were to leave off giving her milk? We should be absolutely reduced to the necessity of killing her, to provide needful meat. He then explained to me in specific detail the manner in which the flesh must be butchered and preserved from spoiling.

Must I then be reduced to such a cruel extreme?

January 26th —

If things do not grow worse, I may be free from anxiety. Blanchette still gives me enough milk for my daily food. I cannot make any more cheese, it is true; but I have yet some in store. I have examined into what remains of other matters, and I have passed the whole day in calculating how long they will last without reckoning upon any thing else. This will not be more than a fortnight.

January 27th —

The milk decreases, and my goat fattens in proportion. So, in case the milk should entirely fail, the poor beast is preparing her self to feed me with her own flesh.

January 30th —

My mind is occupied with one constant and harrowing thought; shall I be reduced to the necessity of becoming the butcher of Blanchette? Shall I be compelled, in order to sustain my sorrowful life, to cut the throat of the animal which has hitherto supported me? I have now no more than half an allowance of milk.

February 1st —

Yesterday the milk had not decreased, but that cost me something. I had given my goat a triple measure of salt, she had drunk more; I discovered it in milking her. Unhappily it will be impossible for me to go on in this manner, for if I am obliged to kill my poor Blanchette, the salt will be absolutely necessary. Kill Blanchette!

Today I have been more economical with the salt, and in consequence have had much less milk.

February 2nd —

I have heard it said, that fowls, if they are too well fed and too much fattened, lay fewer eggs; and I conceived the idea this morning of reducing the quantity of hay that I give Blanchette, thinking it might produce s similar effect. It has not succeeded. Having less nourishment, she has given even less milk than the day before; and I have gained nothing but the pain of hearing her bleating most sorrowfully for more than half the day.

February 3rd —

I have made a new experiment, quite as unsuccessful as that of yesterday. I tried to make Blanchette eat straw instead of hay, thinking that perhaps this change of regimen might make a change in the effects of the nourishment. The goat has only yield ed to my wishes with the greatest difficulty, and, whether out of spite or from suffering, has scarcely given me more than a few drops of milk.

February 4th —

I will torment her no more; if I must kill her, I will render her existence as agreeable as I can to the last moment. Today she has been fed plentifully, and in consequence has been a better nurse. But I have little hopes that this will last; I had better leave nature to itself. After having done my best to avoid a cruel alternative, I must try to submit to it.

February 7th —

In vain I pray as well as work. God, it seems, answers me not; he knows better than I do what is proper for me, and I resign myself to his Divine will. Would it become me to murmur when I behold the calm tranquility of this poor beast which I am going to make my victim? Should the gift of reason be a less effectual for me than the lack of foresight in the poor brute is for her?

It is not now worth while to milk Blanchette twice a day. I waited till the evening in the hope of obtaining a larger quantity at a time, but she will hardly allow me to come near her. I cause her pain in the operation of milking; instinct teaches her that I am treating her improperly; she draws back, and refuses me the little that she has yet to give. Alas! I weary her with my attempts; only because I wish to spare her that blow which she does not expect.

February 8th —

I will own my weakness; I shed tears today when I made a last vain attempt to milk Blanchette, and to ask of her the tribute which she has so long paid me. When she saw me stop she gave me a look of defiance, as if she was standing on her guard against any further attempt. I then threw away my pail; I sat down near the poor beast, embraced her, and wept bitterly.

She continued to munch her food all the same, which she mingled with occasional bleatings and fond looks. They say that a goat distinguishes no one, and that she never shows that jealous and devoted affection which is seen in the dog; but, after all, Blanchette loves her companion, and trusts to him; she seems to expect from me her food and all the little attentions I have bestowed upon her; and must I then plunge a knife in her throat? I shall make her suffer, too, being inexperienced, and I shall see her defending herself against me. God has given the beasts to man for his food as I well know; but it is no offense to Him to attach oneself to those which have been of great service to us, and which He has endowed with such an attractive gentleness; I shall refrain then as long as possible from this cruel sacrifice. I have yet provisions enough left for some days, and I will be as sparing of them as I can.

February 12th —

It is impossible for me to keep my journal regularly in the midst of so many troubles. My food diminishes; I cannot reduce myself to a lower diet without risking my life. Blanchette, who grows daily more fat, seems to offer me better food: that ought to rejoice me, yet I never caressed her so much, and I am making the necessity to which I shall soon be reduced, more painful everyday.

February 13th —

I have been searching all the house over and over again; I have even examined the ground in many places, to discover, if possible, any hidden provisions; I have only in creased my hunger by these exertions. The very idea of being now unable to satisfy it renders it, I believe, daily more acute.

I have said to myself, "After a short time, perhaps, Blanchette's milk will return." Appearances do not favor this supposition; her udder, so swollen and so full some time ago, has shrunk almost to nothing; however I made one more attempt to get a few drops of milk, but in vain.

February 17th —

The cold has become so intense since yesterday evening that I am obliged to keep up a constant fire; certainly, with this temperature, I shall not fear shutting up the flesh of my poor victim in the stable when it freezes very hard without any other precaution; but the weather may grow milder. I must decide then without delay as I have just salt enough to preserve the meat.

February 18th —

The cold is most severe; it has reminded me of the wolves. Nothing now can prevent them from running over the mountain. My God, in this sad condition, it is the only death I fear. If it were thy pleasure to direct an avalanche to swallow me up this day, I should regard death as a deliverance.

February 20th —

I have taken a grand resolution. I will leave the châlet tomorrow. I will write in my journal, which I will leave upon the table, how I came to decide upon this measure.

Yesterday morning, Blanchette's bleatings awoke me from a frightful dream. I thought that I was, with bloody hands, cutting up the quivering limbs of this poor animal; her head lay before me, and yet I still heard the most mournful bleatings proceed from her throat. These, indeed, I heard in reality. I awoke with the tears running down my cheeks. What a pleasure it was to see Blanchette still alive! I ran to her, and she fondled me more than usual. My happiness did not last long as I reflected that my food would be gone in only two days; I had to make up my mind. I took a knife, and sharpened it on the hearth. I was absolutely in despair; it seemed as if I was about to commit murder; and, after staggering forward to strike the fatal blow, I stopped, stung with remorse.

My hands were numbed with cold; this was a reason for delaying an act which caused me so much repugnance. I lighted a good fire, and began to debate with myself as I sat before it. "If the wolves can walk upon the snow," I thought suddenly to myself, "why should not I walk on it too?"

This idea made my heart leap for joy, then fear took its place. I shall go and give myself up to these ravenous beasts; and to avoid feeding upon Blanchette, I shall expose myself to become the prey of wolves!

"And if I kill my goat," I said to myself afterwards, "am I so sure that her flesh will last till the day of my rescue? I have sometimes seen the Jura quite white till the summer; let me not then lose the opportunity which offers itself, while the snow is frozen.

"An attack from wolves on our road is by no means a certainty; for I once set out on the journey, our pace will be rapid; we will go down in a sled."

I leaped up at this thought. My resolution was taken, and from that moment I worked hard to put execute my plan.

Two days sufficed for the construction of the crude sled that was necessary for our journey. I devoted to this purpose the best wood that I had remaining. I made the bases of the sled very broad, to prevent it from sinking in the snow. I mean to fasten my goat on the hinder part, and to tie her legs so that she cannot move; I shall place myself in front. Accustomed, in the sports of my childhood, to guide a sled down steep declines, I hope, if no accident should happen, to make haste off the slopes.

I am going to bed, however, not unmoved. I look with affection upon this prison, where I have suffered so much, and where I must leave my grandfather's remains. I am fearful when I think upon the distance which separates me from the village; but I will not be daunted. The sled is prepared; here is the cord with which I will tie Blanchette's feet; here is the straw which will furnish her both a bed and shelter; the blanket in which I shall wrap myself, and, lastly, the *Imitation of Jesus Christ*. From *that* I will never part; it shall go with me everywhere, in life or death. The last words I shall speak at the moment of my departure from this earth, shall I repeat from it.

"Lord! I am come to this hour, in order that thy glory may be made known, who having so severely afflicted, art now about, as I trust, to deliver me out of my trouble! May it please thee, O Lord, to complete this deliverance; for, weak as I am, what can I do, or where can I go without thee? Help me, O God, and I shall fear nothing, through Jesus Christ our Lord."

March 2nd —

In my father's house.

I am with father again; he has just read my journal a second time, which I had no occasion to leave in the châlet, and he has urged me to finish it. The hurry of spirits in which I still remain, after a week of happiness, will scarcely allow me to relate with much regularity the last scene of my captivity. Everything turned out quite different from what I expected.

On the 24th of February, the cold appeared to me severer than ever; I resolved therefore not to lose a moment. It was necessary to open a sufficient passage for the sled; but I could now throw the snow into the châlet, which made the work much easier. Once I began I proceeded with such eagerness that I soon became tired. I was obliged to take a short rest, during which I lighted the fire.

Scarcely had the smoke begun to ascend, when I heard a great noise without. My first thought was that the wolves had found me out, and were coming to devour me. I shut the door hastily. My fears were soon dissipated; I distinctly heard my name being called out, and I thought I recognized the voice. I replied with all my might. Cries of joy proved that I had been heard.

Immediately a cacophony of voices arose near the door, like the sound of a group urging one another on at some urgent work. After what seemed like merely a few minutes, an opening sufficiently large enough for my exit completed the work I had begun.

My father scarcely could wait till the passage was practicable; and as soon as he could fit he rushed into the châlet with a loud cry and embraced me in his strong arms.

"And your grandfather?" he asked. I was too much affected to form any words and could only lead him into the dairy. He threw himself on his knees upon the grave and I did the same. After some time I endeavored to relate minutely the detail of what had transpired, but he saw by my emotion that the attempt was beyond any strength within me.

"Another time, dear child," he said. "We must not expose ourselves to a new misfortune. Time presses; our return will not be easy."

The men who accompanied him had entered; they were my two uncles, and our servant Pierre.

They all embraced me. They saw my preparations, which were much approved. They determined to set out instantly. My deliverers had placed under their feet pieces of wood armed with small spikes. They had brought two other pieces. Alas! one of them was useless; I put on the other.

Pierre had the charge of the sled. The wolves might come now if they pleased; we were all armed. My father took my hand, and placed a light gun on my shoulder.

"This is not the time," he said, "to remove my father's remains. We will return for them when the season permits, and pay the last duties to him at the village."

"That," I replied, "was my grandfather's own wish." We then entered the dairy for a moment; my uncles being with us. After some moments of silence,

"Adieu!" said my father, overcome with grief. "I fulfill your wishes, I am sure, in taking this dear child away from here as soon as possible; he has caused as much anxiety to you as to us. Adieu, my father!"

We departed with the tears in our eyes. The descent was rapid, but fatiguing. I was much dazzled by the light of the sun and the brightness of the snow. The cold was intense, but I did not complain of it; for I owed my preservation to it. Blanchette, too, owed her life to that icy wind which made her shiver on her sled.

After traversing the snow, without any further accident than sinking in it a little now and then, we arrived at the place, still a long way from the village, to which a road had been opened, in order to make an attempt to reach us. I was greatly struck with the immense labor it must have cost; and I under stand that, but for the frost, I could not have been delivered for a long time.

"You would have been set free in the month of December, if the frost had continued," said my father; "but the snow began to thaw, and we had all our labor to do over again. Know, dear Louis, that our neighbors wanted neither charity nor zeal; but there has never been such a fall of snow in the memory of man. Four times the road has been opened, and four times it has been closed again as completely as before."

"Was it closed from the very first day?" I asked.

My father then made me acquainted with a very sad occurrence. He all but perished in coming down the mountain by the falling of a mass of snow: he had been found, apparently in a dying state, at the brink of a ravine, and near him they had picked up my grandfather's staff and my bottle.

My father was carried home, and remained insensible for three days. All this time was lost in searching for us at the bottom of the ravine. When my father recovered his senses it was too late to make any attempt to deliver us, which would indeed have been dangerous, if not impossible, from the very first day.

I need not speak of the agonies of my father, nor of his efforts to save us; they had suffered more in the village than we had in the châlet. All our neighbors ran out to "meet us, and received me with the greatest affection; I blushed for ever having doubted it. Everyone wants to see Blanchette; she is overwhelmed with caresses on my account The choicest hay and the best litter is reserved for her; she will be the most pampered and the happiest goat that ever was.

God has saved my life, and for that I bless his holy name. He has not permitted my grandfather to see his family again; that dear friend, whose loss I deplore, has taught me never to repine at the decrees of Providence. But Providence demands of me nothing beyond resignation, and will not be offended at my regrets. My God, if I love thee, as it is my duty to do, I owe it to him from whom thou hast separated me; make me thy faithful servant, as he was, that, through the merits of my Savior, I may be one day reunited to him in heaven.

YOU'LL ALSO LOVE THESE BOOKS FOR CHILDREN

Available from www.greatchristianbooks.com

In this classic tale of faith by Amy Le Feuvre we find little Milly has been left an orphan after the sudden death of her mother. Of necessity she is sent to live with her uncle, an affirmed bachelor who dislikes children, and considers little girls even more irksome. Milly at once proves bothersome and tries her uncle's patience with her constant concerns for what she calls "probable" sons—her word for wayward young men since she cannot pronounce "prodigal" correctly. Despite this little quirk Milly exhibits a tender heart for God and God's lost ones. She prayerfully seeks God for all his probable sons to return home. As the days go by, her uncle's heart cannot help but warm to his endearing niece who radiates innocence, love and hope. Probable Sons is a delightful story of forgiveness and reconciliation. Can such innocence and love penetrate even the hardest of hearts, perhaps even that of her very probable uncle?

ISBN 978-1610104906 $6.99

This is the heart-warming story of young David Aspinall, a true prodigal, that learns of the mercy and grace of God and the love of family only after his brush with the law and an arduous journey through the wilds of Africa. David, like many young men, believes that life back home with his family is just not exciting enough for him and that he will surely do well by leaving it all behind and seeking his fortune and adventure in far-off exotic lands. He learns too quickly though that the world is not as inviting and agreeable as he imagined. David soon meets with hardship and life-threatening dangers when he finds himself stranded in Africa but God has other plans for David. By His grace, David eventually finds both his God and his way back home to the loving family that has patiently prayed for his safe return. This is a wonderful, life-affirming tale illustrating the goodness of God through the motif of a story which parallels the 32nd Psalm. Your whole family will enjoy the message taught through the story of David Aspinall— *The Wanderer in Africa*.

ISBN 978-1610101004 $7.99

THE MISSION OF GREAT CHRISTIAN BOOKS

The ministry of Great Christian Books was established to glorify The Lord Jesus Christ and to be used by Him to expand and edify the kingdom of God while we occupy and anticipate Christ's glorious return. Great Christian Books will seek to accomplish this mission by publishing Gospel literature which is biblically faithful, relevant, and practically applicable to many of the serious spiritual needs of mankind upon the beginning of this new millennium. To do so we will always seek to boldly incorporate the truths of Scripture, especially those which were largely articulated as a body of theology during the Protestant Reformation of the sixteenth century and ensuing years. We gladly join our voice in the proclamations of—Scripture Alone, Faith Alone, Grace Alone, Christ Alone, and God's Glory Alone!

Our ministry seeks the blessing of our God as we seek His face to both confirm and support our labors for Him. Our prayers for this work can be summarized by two verses from the Book of Psalms:

"...let the beauty of the LORD our God be upon us, And establish the work of our hands for us; Yes, establish the work of our hands." —Psalm 90:17

"Not unto us, O LORD, not unto us, but to your name give glory."
—Psalm 115:1

Great Christian Books appreciates the financial support of anyone who shares our burden and vision for publishing literature which combines sound Bible doctrine and practical exhortation in an age when too few so-called "Christian" publications do the same. We thank you in advance for any assistance you can give us in our labors to fulfill this important mission. May God bless you.

For a catalog of other great
Christian books including
other wholesome books
for children—

contact us in
any of the following ways:

write us at:
Great Christian Books
160 37th Street
Lindenhurst, NY 11757

call us at:
(631) 956-0998

find us online:
www.greatchristianbooks.com

email us at:
mail@greatchristianbooks.com

www.ingramcontent.com/pod-product-compliance
Lightning Source LLC
Chambersburg PA
CBHW031453040426
42444CB00007B/1090